# French Bulldogs

D. Caroline Coile, Ph.D.

**BARRON'S**

# Contents

# The French Connection

Part gargoyle, part elf, part philosopher, part clown—the enigmatic Frenchie is hard to pin down. Her past, too, is hard to trace. Her bulldog roots are obvious, but how she got from working cattle dog to a socialite darling is more of a mystery. It is a mystery that began in ancient times with warrior dogs.

## BULLDOG ROOTS

By classical Greek times, distinct families of dogs were selectively bred for various purposes. One especially valued family was the Mollossian—large, imposing war dogs. These dogs were so valued that Phoenician traders traded them along their shipping routes, where they gave rise to other families of dogs. British Molossians gave rise to the Mastiff family, which was further perfected as warriors, guardians, and workers.

A subtype of Molossians known as Bullenbeissers earned their keep as butcher's dogs, controlling unruly cattle by grabbing them by the snout and hanging on. Bullenbeissers somewhat resembled today's pit bulls, with sturdy bodies and strong jaws. Pride in their dogs' abilities, combined with the belief that torturing a bull before slaughter made its meat more tender, gave rise to bull-baiting contests and exhibitions. Bulldogs were valued for their gameness, that is, how they would continue to fight even if they were mauled by the bull.

In 1835 England outlawed such blood sports. The unemployed Bulldogs dispersed to fill many roles, from covert pit fighters to mild-mannered companions. Bulldogs were already a source of national pride and had been bred for purposes other than bull baiting since at least 1800. Some had been crossed with terriers, some bred for exaggerated appearance, and some even miniaturized. By 1850 miniature Bulldogs were not uncommon in Britain's towns, and by 1860 they could even be found at some of the early dog shows. Most weighed between 16 and 25 pounds (7 and 11 kg), although there were enough that weighed less than 12 pounds (5 kg) that classes were available for them at dog shows.

## THE FRENCH REVOLUTION

Around this same time, many English artisans, displaced by the factories of the Industrial Revolution, found work in France. Many brought with them their small dogs, among them miniature Bulldogs. The dogs earned their keep as vermin catchers, guardians, and companions. The French so admired them that they called for more miniature Bulldogs from England. English breeders were glad to sell them, as they had little market in England for the smaller dogs, especially if their ears happened to be sticking straight up—a trait disliked by the English. The French did not seem to care

how the dog's ears stood. By 1860 the miniatures had become so popular in France that, with the help of dog dealers specializing in exporting them, few miniatures were left in England.

City life: The miniatures, dubbed Bouledogue Francais, moved into the cities, where they became the darlings of Paris prostitutes. No streetwalker's ensemble was complete without a Bouledogue Francais. Avant-garde artists, fashion designers, and writers followed. The Bouledogue became the ultimate fashion statement. French society ladies reveled in showing off their dogs as they rode in their carriages along the busy boulevards.

Record keeping: French dog breeders were not the careful record keepers that

the British were, so the breeding history of these dogs is unknown. It is known that the Bouledogue Francais came to look less bulldoggish than did her English counterpart, probably through crosses with terriers and pugs. These may have produced higher ears, straighter backs, and rounder eyes compared with the original English stock.

Return to England: In 1893 the little dogs came full circle when several were brought back to England. They were not welcomed by English breeders of Bulldogs and Toy Bulldogs because they did not fit the English Bulldog standards. Supporters of both English and French types were concerned that their dogs would be interbred to the detriment of each. Yet the (English) Kennel Club recognized the newcomers as a class of English Bulldogs. Rather than allow their distinctive dogs to be assimilated into the Bulldog mainstream, Bouledogue Francais fanciers formed their own club in 1902. The club's first show was held in 1903 with 51 entries. In 1905 the Kennel Club relented and recognized the dogs as a separate breed, Bouledogue Francais. In 1912, the name was changed to French Bulldog.

## Spanish Blood

Some early breed historians dispute the English roots of the breed, contending instead that the Frenchie was bred down from Spanish Bulldog types, including the Dogue de Bordeaux.

The French Bulldog Club of England was not the first national Frenchie club, however. France, Germany, Austria, and America already had staunch admirers and national French Bulldog clubs. The American club would become one of the most influential for the breed's future shape.

## Frenchie Trivia

- One of the earliest depictions of a French Bulldog in art was painted by the English artist Dean Wolstenholme (1798–1882). The breed has remained a popular artistic subject since.
- A French Bulldog was aboard the Titanic when it sank. The dog, named Gamin de Pycombe, had been bought for the equivalent of $17,000 in today's prices, but went down with the ship. A surviving passenger reported seeing the dog swimming in the ocean.
- Frenchie owners over the years have included Martha Stewart, Leonardo DiCaprio, Reese Witherspoon, Yves Saint Laurent, David and Victoria Beckham, Ashlee Simpson, Michelle Trachtenberg, Hugh Jackman, Nathan Lane, Jason Priestley, John Legend, Renée Felice Smith, Patton Oswalt, Jason Schwartzman, Jonah Hill, David Price, Jeremy Renner, King Edward VII, Prince Albert (Prince of Wales), and the Grand Duchess Tatiana of Russia.
- The French Bulldog is in the AKC Non-Sporting group.
- The Frenchie is currently the 14th most popular AKC breed—up from 58th a decade ago!

## The Boston Bull

Some early reports credited American crosses with the Boston Terrier with streamlining the breed and helping establish the bat ears.

- In 2013, the Frenchie was the second most popular breed (behind the Bulldog) in New York City.
- *Daisy and Josephine* is a children's book about a Frenchie written by Melissa Gilbert.
- The restaurant elBulli in Spain is named for the Catalan term for French Bulldog because it was built on land that once was home to them. The restaurant has been named the "Best Restaurant in the World" five times. In California, there's also a restaurant named The French Bulldog.
- A French Bulldog named Rebecca Bonbon is a character in the Hello Kitty collection.
- A French Bulldog named Stella is a member of the *Modern Family* television show cast.
- A French Bulldog named Blanche is a character in Jonathan Kellerman's Alex Delaware mystery series.

## RED, WHITE, AND BLUE BLOODS

Wealthy Americans traveling in Europe often brought back Bouledogues Francais as souvenirs of their stay. Back in America, the little dogs were a hit among socialites.

Dog breeders became enthralled by the new breed. By 1885 Bouledogues Francais were being brought over from France for breeding purposes. They remained a breed of the social elite. Since the social elite often dabbled in dog showing, not much time passed before the little French dog made her ring debut in the New World. In 1896 some of the who's who of society ladies exhibited 19 French Bulldogs as a special attraction at the Westminster Kennel Club. The following year entries doubled. However, something even more important occurred: all of the judge's winning dogs had rose ears, in which the ear folded, as were preferred by the English and French at that time. So perturbed were the ladies that they called a meeting at which they officially declared the erect bat ear the correct ear for the breed. They drafted a standard for the breed and formed the French Bull Dog Club of America. In 1898 they held their first French Bulldog specialty show, a high-society affair held at the Waldorf-Astoria. It attracted an entry of 50 Frenchies, many exhibited by some of the most prominent ladies of the day.

**AKC recognition:** Every lady or aspiring lady had to have a French Bulldog seated beside her in her carriage or at tea. The dogs' high price tag, up to $3,000, only made them more in vogue. Influential Frenchie-owning families such as the Rockefellers and J. P. Morgans were connected with the American Kennel Club (AKC). They no doubt hastened the breed's AKC recognition, which took only a year

## French Toasts of the Town

✔ In 1898 the French import, Guguss II, became the first AKC-registered French Bulldog.
✔ In 1899 Rico became the first AKC Champion French Bulldog.
✔ In 1905 the French import Ch. Nellcorte Gamin was first exhibited and declared so nearly perfect that he became a stud dog of unparalleled influence.
✔ In 1924 the female Ch. Evergay Charmer became the first Frenchie to win an AKC all-breed Best in Show of significance.
✔ Only one Frenchie–Ch. Robobull Fabelhaft I'm On Fire–has won the group at the Westminster dog show, and none has ever won Best in Show . . . yet.

and a half following that first Westminster exhibition. Recognition further fueled the Frenchie fire. By 1906 the number of entries at Westminster topped 100, and the Frenchie was the fifth most popular breed in America.

**Perfected in America:** By 1907 the American French Bulldog had attained such status that European countries, where the bat ear had never been in particular favor nor highly perfected, adopted the bat ear as the correct ear. It is said that the French Bulldog may have originated in Europe but was perfected in America.

**Becoming rare:** Frenchie numbers continued to grow until stabilizing in the mid-1920s. Eventually, the elitist attitude

of Frenchie owners and even the French Bulldog Club backfired. Newcomers were not welcomed. Frenchie numbers dwindled. Within a short time, they became a relatively rare breed.

A champion: The Frenchie languished in obscurity for decades, cherished by those who knew it but unheard of by most people. Frenchies had their stars, though. In 1951 Ch. Bouquet Nouvelle Ami won 30 Best in Shows. More importantly, Jo-Jo was perhaps the first big-winning, cream-colored Frenchie. Until then, most Frenchies were dark-colored or pied (white with patches of color). In fact, the standards of

some European countries did not recognize creams, so Jo-Jo's success was all the more remarkable. Jo-Jo's cream granddaughter, Ch. Ralandi Ami Francine, was an indomitable force in the show ring, winning 55 Best in Shows and ranking among the top dogs of all breeds for several years. Serious dog fanciers have never ignored the Frenchie.

In recent years, the French Bulldog has made a comeback. Still the darling of those who aspire to the very best, Frenchies will nonetheless make themselves at home in modest accommodations, alternately playing the role of privileged aristocracy and court jester.

# French Kisses

You have a lot to consider before you Frenchify your life. Does the Frenchie really have the right personality for you? Is the breed suited for your climate and lifestyle? Could breed-related health problems be an eventual hardship? Learn about the Frenchie before joining the French Bulldog legions.

# FRANKLY FRENCHIE

The dog of your dreams comes racing when you call him, snuggles close when you are resting, protects you when you are threatened, plays when you are energetic, trots smartly at your side in public, never gets into trouble, and stays out of the way the rest of the time. The dog of your dreams does not exist. However, the Frenchie may come close.

Frenchies will come when called—if nothing else better is going on. They will snuggle up with you on the sofa—just do not sleep all day! They will protect you if you are threatened, maybe—then again, maybe not. They will play when you are energetic—and even beyond that time. They will make you look good in public—unless they are playing the clown. What about never getting into trouble and staying out of the way? Only stuffed animals fit those criteria.

## Temperament

Known as the clown in the robe of a philosopher, Frenchies are both comical and thoughtful. Their imaginative antics sometimes seem out of place with their pensive expression, but that face can express an incredible range of emotions. Spend just a little time with one, and you will be hard pressed not to fall in love with this mighty elf.

**Cute:** For one thing, despite (or maybe because of) that sour mug, Frenchies are cute! Beware: that is how they get away with mischief! No matter how innocent they can appear when it is convenient, remember, they are called French Bulldogs because they have a Bulldog ancestry. Their forefathers (and mothers) were bred to be tenacious and brave, something that translates into stubbornness and mischievousness in the world of pet dogs. Obedience training is a necessity, but any attempt to prove who is boss through sheer force will result in the Frenchie digging in his heels and proving who really rules the house. Frenchies respond far better to teamwork mixed with a little bribery.

**Servants:** Do not expect a Frenchie to be your hand servant; more likely, it will be the other way around. However, if you make a reasonable request, especially if it involves fun, most Frenchies will make a reasonable attempt to humor you.

11

Frenchies are not barky dogs: They usually bark for a reason, such as a burglar who refuses to share any dog treats. If you want a Frenchie as a guard dog, you should also invest in a good home security system. Frenchies can put on a ferocious front when confronted with an intruder, but their barks of warning too often turn into yips of glee at the prospect of a new friend breaking into the house. Still, some Frenchies are good, even excellent, watchdogs. A few Frenchies even try to guard your belongings from you, as well, a habit that must be dealt with early.

Limitations: Being a guard dog is not the only thing for which Frenchies are not known. Although they appreciate a jaunt around the block and offer an impressive sprint around the yard, Frenchies are utter failures as jogging partners. Their stubby legs are not made for repeated pounding. Their flat faces are not made for deep breathing or warm weather.

## French Bulldog Health Concerns

✔ Hemivertebrae
✔ Intervertebral disk disease
✔ Elongated soft palate
✔ Stenotic nares
✔ Atopic dermatitis
✔ Retinal dysplasia
✔ Hip dysplasia
✔ Patellar luxation
✔ Megaesophagus
✔ Cleft palate
See pages 81–85 for more information about these conditions.

Frenchies are even worse swimming partners. Their stocky bodies have the buoyancy of bricks. Frenchies cannot compete in herding, earthdog, racing, or field trials. They do make great show dogs, good obedience dogs, and passable agility dogs. No matter what the event, they have a habit of playing to the audience, usually with comic results.

Unique abilities: It is not what Frenchies cannot do that sets them apart—it is what they can do. They can cuddle, entertain, and love without equal. They are romantics, adventurers, and clowns. If a Frenchie cannot bring a smile to your face or brighten your mood, nobody can. They are unsurpassed as therapy dogs. Other breeds live to hunt or herd or work; Frenchies live to love. Nothing is more important to their happiness than the chance to be with their special people, whether just relaxing on the couch, playing in the yard, or driving in the car. They will follow you from room to room, reveling in your most mundane tasks.

Frenchies love to play, and they will gladly throw themselves into a rough-and-tumble game with anyone who will humor them. They make great companions for children, as long as the children are equally great companions to them. Even Frenchies have their limits, and they will do their best to avoid rough or careless children. Frenchies can get underfoot. They are also easy to drop because their heavy front end makes their center of balance more forward than anticipated. Small children should never try to carry a Frenchie. Frenchies may be too rambunctious for very small children.

Sense of self: Some Frenchies believe they should be the only dog in the house, if not the universe. This is especially true of unspayed females, who may quarrel with other females. Frenchies generally get along better with dogs of the opposite sex, and they also tend to be more amiable if they are spayed or neutered. Frenchies can live quite peacefully with cats, especially if they are raised with cats. However, the peace may be interrupted occasionally by a gleeful chase around the house. Nobody is perfect.

## Upkeep

Frenchies can be at home in town or country—inside, of course. They cannot live outside. The conformation of their head and respiratory system makes them extremely prone to overheating, and their close coat makes them prone to chilling. They are not all-season dogs. Although they appreciate the chance to frolic outside on temperate days, you must always be watchful that they are not overtaxing themselves. They must always have access to cool shelter and water. Rethink getting a Frenchie if you live in a warm climate and do not have air-conditioning. Better yet, get air-conditioning!

Frenchies crave the good life: If there was a doggy lifestyle of the rich and famous, Frenchies would plan on starring in every episode. However, the humblest abodes can be transformed into a French chalet, as long as it is shared with loved ones. Frenchies make excellent apartment dogs.

The Frenchie coat is short and smooth, easy to care for, and just right for stroking. Their kissably cute noses can tend to dry out, crack, and scale unless occasionally treated to a coat of petroleum jelly or vitamin E. The wrinkle above the muzzle must be cleaned regularly and kept dry to avoid bacterial infections. Their eyes, ears, and teeth are no more difficult to care for than any dog's. Frenchies are not droolers, but they are snorers, snufflers, and

## The Bull Market

French Bulldogs are expensive. The current price range for a companion-quality puppy usually runs to four figures. Show-quality dogs cost even more. Their expense is not a plot among breeders to keep prices high but instead reflects the costs of raising a difficult breed. Most Frenchie breedings must be done by artificial insemination and delivered by caesarean section. Litters tend to be small. Neonatal mortality can be high unless the dam and pups are monitored carefully in the early days. This makes the breeder's investment per puppy substantially higher than in most breeds.

Do not fall for the recent ruse of foreign-bred imports being offered at cheap prices. These puppies are raised under poor conditions, separated from their dams at too early an age, and brought en masse to America by puppy brokers.

wheezers. They are also gifted gas passers. If you are easily disturbed by noises and odors of bodily functions, maybe a Frenchie is not for you.

Size: Whether you like a big dog or a little dog, Frenchies can fit the bill. Frenchie males usually weigh from 24 to 28 pounds (10 to 13 kg) and females from 19 to 24 pounds (8 to 10 kg). These are sturdy, compact dogs with strong bodies. They are small enough to take almost anywhere conveniently, yet large enough to avoid being stepped on or easily injured. They have a Bulldog-type conformation but with less exaggeration. This makes them less prone to conformation-associated problems as com-

pared with Bulldogs. However, the prospective Frenchie owner still needs to be acquainted with some Frenchie health concerns.

## Health

The very traits that make Frenchies so appealing can also make them more prone to some health problems, particularly breathing difficulties and overheating. Frenchies are a brachycephalic breed, which means they have flat faces with short muzzles. This configuration also means they have compacted respiratory systems, which lead to a condition called brachycephalic syndrome. It consists of a group of anatomical abnormalities that may lead to breathing problems. These problems range from the Frenchie's amusing snorting and snuffling repertoire to exercise intolerance to life-threatening breathing difficulties. Problems associated with breathing difficulties are one of the major causes of death in French Bulldogs. These difficulties entail special anesthesia risks as well.

Frenchies are also heat intolerant: Dogs build up heat according to body mass and give off heat according to body surface. The Frenchie's heavy, chunky body has a minimal amount of body surface compared with body mass and tends to hold heat more than the average dog. Dogs rid themselves of excess heat by evaporation from the tongue and respiratory tract surfaces. The Frenchie's face, muzzle, and respiratory tract have relatively little surface area available for cooling. Frenchies build up heat and cannot shed it, making them at grave risk of deadly heatstroke in even mild weather. All French Bulldog owners must be prepared to shield their dogs from overheating.

Other Frenchie health concerns include back, knee, hip, and allergy problems. See pages 81–85 for more detailed descriptions of Frenchie concerns. Before you run away in a panic, French Bulldogs would be extinct if these problems were rampant. Overheating, followed by back and breathing problems, are the main concerns. By knowing what problems to look for, you can better ensure—although not guarantee—that your Frenchie will be one of the healthy ones.

## FINDING YOUR FRENCHIE FRIEND

Now that you have chosen the French Bulldog as your breed, the time has come to take the same care in choosing your own special French Bulldog. Although you could find a French Bulldog in the newspaper, a pet store, or on the Internet with little effort, why would you consider choosing a family member with

### Breeder Listings

AKC Breeder Classified:
*www.akc.org/classified*

French Bulldog Club of America Breeder Listing Service:
*www.frenchbulldogclub.org/about-frenchies/breeder-listing*

so little care? It is worth the effort to find a Frenchie that embodies the best this breed has to offer. Remember the traits that attracted you to the French Bulldog: his looks and personality. Remember also the all-important trait of good health.

Looks: You want your French Bulldog to look like a French Bulldog, so make sure his parents have at least the essence of the Frenchie appearance: a frog face, bat ears, and a stocky, compact body. If you simply want a

Frenchie as a companion, you need not concern yourself with the finer points of conformation. If you have aspirations of entering the show ring, you will need to study the standard (page 60), visit dog shows, and talk to breeders. You will want to make sure your Frenchie show-dog-to-be has a champion-studded pedigree, with at least one parent holding the title of Champion.

**Personality:** Finding a Frenchie with a poor personality is hard, but why take chances? Try to meet both parents to make sure they have the sort of temperament you want in your Frenchie. The typical Frenchie is outgoing and vivacious. Think again about choosing a dog from shy or potentially aggressive parents. If you dream of trying obedience competition with your Frenchie, you can hedge your bet by getting one from a family of dogs that has proven their obedience aptitude by earning obedience titles (see page 51).

**Health:** The best indicator of your prospective Frenchie's health is the health of not just his parents but his aunts, uncles, grandparents, and any other family members. How long did they live? What did they die of? What sort of health screening tests did they have? What health problems did they have? Did they require medical or surgical treatment to live comfortably? A dog that needed surgery for elongated soft palate, cleft palate, stenotic nares, megaesophagus, or tracheal collapse usually should not be bred, and you should avoid getting an offspring from such a dog.

If only health screening tests were available for every possible Frenchie disorder. Unfortunately, they are not. Even if they were available, not every breeder would use them. Give high marks to breeders who test breeding stock and puppies for as many disorders as possible. Give low marks to breeders who claim Frenchies have no health problems or that their line has never had a health problem—unless they can offer evidence in the form of health certifications proving the latter.

## Good Breeders

Responsible French Bulldog breeders do not sell puppies except to people they have interviewed. That means that puppies advertised through stores or third parties probably are not from good breeders. Because French Bulldogs command high prices, some unethical breeders churn out as many litters as they can, cutting as many corners as possible in hopes of turning a profit. Their puppies come from parents with no health testing or health care and are raised in deplorable conditions with no socialization. If you cannot see photos of at least the sire and dam, you are probably not getting a puppy that was bred with quality and health as a priority. Even though you simply want a companion, it is in your best interest to buy from a responsible breeder who breeds for quality Frenchies. Such breeders usually have companion-quality dogs that look just as beautiful, have just as good personalities, are just as healthy, and have been raised with the same love and care as their next Best in Show prospect.

Look for responsible breeders exhibiting at dog shows, especially French Bulldog specialty shows. The French Bulldog Club of

### Breeder Checklist

Responsible breeders:
✔ Breed only one or two breeds of dogs so they can concentrate on just those breeds.
✔ Breed no more than three or four litters per year so they can concentrate on those litters.
✔ Can compare their dogs objectively with the French Bulldog standard.
✔ Can discuss French Bulldog health concerns and provide evidence of the health of their own dogs.
✔ Can give substantial reasons relating to quality of conformation, temperament, and health about why they bred the litter or chose those parents.
✔ Have pictures of several generations of the puppy's ancestors.
✔ Have clean, friendly, healthy adults.
✔ Have clean facilities that promote interaction with their dogs.
✔ Raise their litter inside the house and underfoot, not in a kennel or garage.
✔ Question you about your facilities, your prior experiences with dogs, and your intentions regarding your new dog.
✔ Sell companion-quality puppies with only AKC limited registration, which means their progeny cannot be registered.
✔ Insist upon taking the dog back should you be unable to keep him at any time during his life.

America (*www.fbdca.org*) maintains a breeder listing service on their website that lists only their members who agree to adhere to their Code of Ethics. If you want a show dog, subscribe to the award-winning *French Bullytin*

17

puppies more vulnerable to the possibility of stress-related disorders.

## Breeders to Avoid

- Avoid breeders who offer Frenchies of so-called rare colors, such as merle. Merles (which have irregular dark splotches of hair laid over a grayish background) are not in the purebred Frenchie gene pool and are probably the result of crossing with other breeds (very likely Chihuahuas). Other colors offered as rare include solid black, black and white, gray, liver, or black with tan points.
- Avoid breeders who deal in designer dogs that are part Frenchie. Such breeders often tout imaginary health benefits, but few do health testing and the dogs are very often not as healthy as purebreds—especially because such breeders are often motivated mostly by cashing in on the designer dog fad.
- Avoid breeders who work through brokers or middle men. A good breeder will demand to know you personally.
- Avoid Frenchies imported from other countries. Except for the highest caliber show dogs, these dogs are usually mass-produced under horrible conditions that are exempt from AKC or USDA inspection.
- Avoid Frenchies registered with any but the AKC or UKC (in America). Other registries register anything.
- Avoid breeders who sell from online "Puppies for Sale" sites—or at the very least, check them out extremely carefully. Good breeders have their own websites and referral networks.
- Avoid puppies from pet stores, which come from large-scale puppy mills.

magazine, where you will find pictures of dogs and advertisements of puppies from responsible breeders around the country. *Just Frenchies* magazine also includes pictures of top show dogs.

Waiting: Once you have made up your mind, you are naturally going to be in a hurry to get your new Frenchie. However, good breeders have waiting lists for puppies. Even if they happen to have one available, good breeders do not let French Bulldog puppies leave for new homes until they are 10 to 12 weeks old and weigh at least 8 or even 10 pounds (3.6 to 4.5 kg). The stress of changing homes makes small

## Rescue

Responsible breeders provide a home for their Frenchies for life should their new owners not be able to keep them. Unfortunately, not all Frenchies are bred by responsible breeders. Even responsible breeders sometimes have unforeseen circumstances and cannot take back a dog. Frenchies end up in rescue for many reasons. Perhaps they were lost and never claimed, perhaps their owners died, or perhaps their owners could not afford them or simply tired of having a dog. Whatever the reason, these dogs are filled with love but have no one on whom to lavish it. Occasionally, they have behavior problems often stemming from poor training or socialization. However, good rescue organizations will make sure you know any problems ahead of time and will help you guide your Frenchie to becoming the best dog he can be. Rescue Frenchies range from puppies to seniors but have in common a need for a forever home they can call their own. Check out page 92 for some French Bulldog rescue groups.

## WHICH BULLY FOR YOU?

As you look upon a throng of bouncing baby bulls—how will you ever choose? In most cases, you should let the breeder choose. The breeder will know more about the puppies' personalities and which are better destined to be show dogs or obedience dogs. You do need to tell the breeder about any preferences you have, though.

**Sex:** Have you considered males versus females? In Frenchies, the difference is not great. The males are a bit larger, and some Frenchie owners consider males a bit more loving. The females will come into estrus twice a year and can make a mess of your rugs unless you have them spayed. If you already have a dog, often the best choice is a dog of the opposite sex—as long as you plan to neuter and spay them.

**Color:** What about color? Frenchies come in more colors than you might think. The standard allows all-brindle, brindle and white, all-fawn, all-white, and any color except those that

are specifically disqualified. The disqualified colors are solid black (black without a trace of brindle), mouse, liver, black and tan, black and white, and white with black.

Seal or black brindle is a very dark brindle, appearing almost black. Tiger brindle is black brindling over a lighter, often reddish background, with or without a black mask. Both brindle colors can be solid or combined

with varying amounts of white. Mostly white dogs are called pied. Brindling can also appear diluted or blue. Cream can range from very pale to fawn.

Dogs of disqualified colors cannot be shown but make beautiful companions. However, breeders should not purposefully breed for them, and any breeder who touts them as rare or expensive should be eyed with suspicion.

**Health:** Good health is essential. You should make any sale contingent on a veterinary exam performed within three days. Before getting attached to any puppy, give him a quick health check.

- The skin should not have parasites, hair loss, crusts, or reddened areas.
- The eyes, ears, and nose should be free of discharge.
- The puppy should not be coughing, sneezing, or vomiting and neither should any of his companion puppies.
- The area around the anus should have no hint of irritation or recent diarrhea.
- The puppy should be neither thin nor potbellied.
- The gums should be pink, not pale.
- The eyelids and lashes should not fold in on the eyes.
- By the age of 12 weeks, both of a male's testicles should have descended into the scrotum.
- Avoid any puppy that is making significant breathing sounds, including excessive wheezing or snorting.
- Avoid any puppy with pinched nostrils, especially if they appear to collapse inward when the dog inhales.
- Avoid any puppy with a curved back or with signs of pain or paralysis.
- Avoid any puppy with a tail that is recessed.

**Conformation:** An experienced breeder has great difficulty picking a show prospect puppy; it is impossible for an inexperienced novice to pick one! If you want a show prospect, trust the breeder to choose for you. If you want a companion, choose the puppy that looks the most like a miniature French Bulldog. Make sure the puppy moves freely with no signs of lameness and that the teeth are not crooked or crowded. Frenchies are one of the few breeds in which the bite should be undershot. This means the incisors (front teeth) of the bottom jaw protrude in front of those of the upper jaw. This should be apparent even in puppies, although it need not be pronounced. The head should already have a frog face expression and erect bat ears. The body should be chunky.

**Temperament:** It is hard not to be impressed with the pup that is a little spitfire or want to nurture the one who shyly hangs back. Unless you have a fondness for naughty dogs or one-person dogs, you will do better to pick the pup that plays a little, comes to say "Hi," then never leaves your lap. Face it, in most litters, it is hard not to try to fit every pup into your car and take them all home. However, if you do not see the pup of your dreams, tell the breeder. A good breeder only wants you to leave with a puppy that has captured your heart. Of course, that is not hard—what Frenchie would not?

# Growing Up Frenchie

What a difference a year makes. This will be your Frenchie's wonder year, and the way you handle it will make a huge difference in your future together. There is so much to do in so little time. . . .

## BRING IN THE CLOWN

Can your home withstand a fractious French fry? Getting ready for a new puppy is harder than getting ready for a new baby. A baby will stay confined to a crib for a while, but your Frenchie will be raring to go as soon as she comes home. She will outdo any baby in her ability to gnaw, dig, and cause general chaos. So get up and get puppy proofing!

How can you possibly get everything out of your Frenchie's reach? You can either throw away everything you own and live in an empty husk of a home, or you can confine your pup to small, Frenchie-proofed areas. Chances are the area will not be the garage since that is a haven for most of your poisons. It will not be the bathroom since that room holds many dangerous items and also tends to be claustrophobic for a pup. The kitchen can be a problem since your pup will be trying to trip you while you cook. You need a small playpen, or exercise pen, available from pet supply catalogs, that you can place on a waterproof floor in a safe room that you are in a lot. You also need a crate, available from most pet supply stores, that your pup can use as her private bedroom. If you place the crate in the exercise pen (X-pen), you can have a tiny, safe, indoor yard for your dog when you have to be out of the house.

A crate is not a cruel punishment. However, it can begin to seem so if you use it as a storage box for your dog. Frenchies are not stuffed animals that can be locked away when they are inconvenient. They are social butterflies. They need interaction, exercise, and stimulation. Teach your Frenchie to like her crate by placing her into it when she begins to fall asleep. Give her a treat in it. Most of all, do not overuse it.

## HOUSETRAINING

Puppies have simple pleasures—chewing, playing, snuggling, and eating. High on the list are peeing and pooping. These actions are self-rewarding because emptying a full bladder or bowel feels good. The more any behavior is rewarded, the more likely it will recur. That means the very act of pottying in a particular place makes her more likely to potty there again. Add to that the powerful olfactory cues of her own urine and

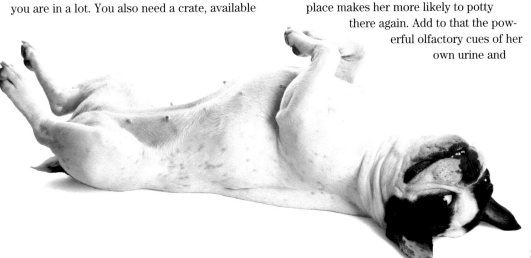

feces that scream out "Here's your bathroom!" and you can see how vital it is that you prevent her from having those indoor accidents right from the start.

Unfortunately, circumstances conspire against you. If she was raised indoors she has already had plenty of rewarding experiences pottying inside. There is a lot to be said for comfort and convenience. That is why people have indoor plumbing. Then there is the social aspect. You would not expect to potty train a child by just plopping him onto a toilet and walking away. Do not expect to potty train your puppy by shoving her out the door and walking away. If you do, she will huddle by the door until she can be reunited with you and then rush inside and potty on the floor. Instead, no matter how rushed you are or how daunting the weather is, go outside with her. When she

potties outside, praise her and give her a treat just as you would for any other trick you would teach her. Do not wait until she is back inside; then it is too late.

Control issues: Young puppies have poor bladder and bowel control. A rule of thumb is that a puppy can hold herself for as many hours as the pup is months old. That means a two-month old can wait for two hours, a four-month old for four hours, up to about six months old. Always take her out before her regularly scheduled program of peeing or pooping. Also get her outside as soon as she awakens, soon after she eats, in the middle of playing, or any time you see her sniffing or circling.

If you are like most people and cannot devote all your time to following your pup constantly, you can make use of a canine's natural desire to keep her own den clean. That means

## Puppy Proofing 101

Fill in the following checklist:

Check all over for
- [ ] uncovered electrical outlets
- [ ] open stairways, decks, or balconies
- [ ] unsecured doors

Check the kitchen for
- [ ] open cabinets holding cleaners and degreasers
- [ ] accessible garbage pails holding enticing rancid food and splintering bones
- [ ] pan handles extending invitingly over stovetop edges
- [ ] plastic wraps that can become lodged in the intestines

Check the dining room for
- [ ] hanging tablecloths that, if pulled, can bring dishes crashing down
- [ ] swinging doors that can trap a puppy's head and neck

Check the family room for
- [ ] a fireplace without a secure fire screen
- [ ] unsteady bookcases
- [ ] craft or sewing kits
- [ ] heavy statues or vases

Check the bedrooms for
- [ ] children's toys
- [ ] open closets, especially shoe closets

Check the bathrooms for
- [ ] pills and medicines
- [ ] hair treatments
- [ ] drain cleaners
- [ ] toilets with open lids
- [ ] razors
- [ ] diaper pails

Check the garage for
- [ ] antifreeze
- [ ] fuels, cleaners, paints—just about anything in a can
- [ ] batteries
- [ ] nails and screws
- [ ] herbicides, insecticides, or fertilizers
- [ ] rodent bait

Check the yard for
- [ ] a weak fence
- [ ] rotted limbs
- [ ] an unfenced pool
- [ ] cocoa mulch
- [ ] nut trees
- [ ] pointed sticks at eye level
- [ ] predators
- [ ] treated lawns
- [ ] poisonous plants
- [ ] insect hives

## The 60/40 Rule

Because Frenchies are so front heavy, if you pick them up like you would another dog, they would topple forward out of your arms. Instead, distribute your Frenchie's weight so you are supporting her around midchest, with about 60 percent of her length behind and 40 percent in front. Of course, you should also steady your Frenchie with your other hand.

she will avoid soiling her crate if she has come to know it as her bed. If she is in the crate, she will learn to hold herself until you let her out, as long as you do not make unreasonable demands. As she gets better at controlling herself, you can gradually enlarge her personal space. Start by placing her bed or crate into a tiny enclosed area—an area only a very short distance beyond the boundary of her bed. Be especially vigilant so you can prevent her from soiling this area. Once she goes several days without soiling her area, make it just a little bit larger and then larger.

A doggy door: If you cannot be home to take her out as often as she needs to go, consider installing a doggy door that leads to a safe outdoor area. Enclose just enough indoor area so she can get from her crate to the door. Puppies catch on to doggy doors quickly, and you can boast your dog has her own French door.

If you do not have a doggy door option, you may have to resort to indoor plumbing. You can opt for the old newspaper standby, but be forewarned that soiled newspapers smell horribly. Better than paper are absorbent pee pads—although pups like to rip

them up. Some people have success with sod squares; after all, that is what you are trying to teach her to use outside. When the squares are soiled, just plant them and look forward to a newly sodded yard by the time she is house-trained. Either way, start by covering the entire area, and gradually reduce the size of coverage so the dog is aiming just for the paper or sod. Be warned: Some puppies just try to dig in the sod! You may also consider one of the indoor potty areas made for dogs, especially if she may need to use one as an adult.

When accidents occur: In the ideal world, you will never once miss the warning signs and your Frenchie will never once potty inside. Your world is not ideal. You will miss signs, and your dog will have accidents. If you catch her in the act, pick her up quickly and whisk her outside. If you do not see her doing it, you can do nothing. She was not being sneaky or spiteful, and she will have no idea what your problem is if you start yelling and pointing. Such behavior will only convince her that every once in a while, for no apparent reason, you go insane. Rubbing her nose in her mess will simply further convince her of your perverted nature.

Cleaning a mess: Puppy owners learn the secrets of carpet cleaning fast. Pick and soak up as much of the deposit as possible. Then add a little water and again soak up as much as possible. If you have a rug cleaner that extracts liquid, now is the time to use it. If you do not, buy one. Next apply an enzyme digester type odor neutralizer (these are products specifically made for dog accidents); use enough to penetrate the pad. Leave it on for a long time, following directions. Cover the area with plastic so it does not dry out before the digester can break down the urine. The final step is to add a nice odor, such as a mixture of lavender oil or vanilla with baking soda, to the area. Let it air out, then vacuum.

**When will it ever end?** That depends. It depends on how your Frenchie was raised before you got her, how diligent you have been, and how she just happens to take to the idea. A few gifted dogs are housetrained by three months of age, but five or six months is far more common. If your Frenchie appears to urinate abnormally frequently, have your veterinarian check her for a urinary tract infection. Be forewarned: Frenchies tend to take longer than most breeds to master the art of pottying outside.

## FIRST LESSONS

Your Frenchie's wonder months are the time she will be learning about the world and her place in it. The lessons she learns now will shape her social life for years to come. Frenchies begin life relatively fearless but gradually become more cautious with age. Eventually, they become suspicious of novel situations and objects, adjusting to them with greater difficulty. The secret is to expose your pup to as much as possible while she is too young to be afraid. Then when she meets the same experience later in life, she will already know it is nothing to fear. That means exposing her to men, women, children, dogs, cats, traffic, stairs, noises, grooming, leash walking, crates, and alone time.

**Proceed carefully:** Not so fast! Exposing does not mean overwhelming. A bad experience is worse than no experience. Good experiences are low stress and involve lots of rewards. Exposing your pup to other dogs also entails a chance of exposing her to disease. Until your pup is at least 12 weeks old and has had two sets of puppy vaccinations, you should avoid exposing her to strange dogs or places lots of dogs frequent.

**If you already have another dog,** you should introduce your new Frenchie carefully. Let them meet by walking on lead together in neutral territory. Since your puppy probably does not know how to walk on lead yet, that

may not be possible. In that case, keep the older dog on lead, but do not allow the pup to maul him. Your other dog may take a week or so to warm up to this pesky intruder. Make sure your older dog always gets fed and petted first, and let him know he is still number one with you. Lock the pup away if need be so your older dog gets special time with you. Feed him special treats so he comes to associate the puppy with good times. Your pup will naturally revere him as a minor deity. Your older dog may have to give the youngster some warning growls or snaps to keep her out of his hair. Let him mildly reprimand her if she is out of hand, but try to remove her from him so the situation does not progress to that point.

Introduce the family cat in a similar way, except let them meet indoors where the cat can get out of the way. The cat is more likely to have the winning edge, so you may have to crate the pup at first for her own safety. Frenchies and cats can become close friends, but that is mostly up to the cat!

Children are drawn to cute Frenchie puppies, so be sure your pup is not mobbed by a crowd of puppy petters. Let your pup meet children one by one, with both child and pup on the ground. That way the pup cannot be stepped on or dropped. Children must be taught that puppies cannot be handled roughly. Dogs and young children should always be supervised for the well-being of both. Dogs and babies should also be supervised. Always make a fuss over the dog when the baby is around so the dog will associate the baby with good times.

Alone time: Do not forget to accustom your puppy to being alone. Dogs are not naturally loners, and being alone is very stressful for them. This must be done gradually, so your puppy knows you are coming back soon. Give her special interactive chew toys that you give her only when you are leaving so she will have something to occupy her. Despite your efforts, many dogs will develop separation anxiety. See page 44 for tips on coping with that potentially serious behavioral problem.

## House Rules

The typical new puppy scenario goes like this: The baby pup is placed onto the sofa, the bed, and everybody's lap because she is so cute! As she gets older and wilder, one day the owners remember that dogs do not belong on the furniture. So they embark on a cold-turkey furniture withdrawal for the pup. The pup cannot grasp this bizarre change in the rules of the universe and continues to get onto the furniture. If the owner is adamant enough, the pup learns to get onto the furniture only when the crazy furniture police person is out of the room. This charade continues for the next 10 years—or however long is necessary before the owner relents and lets her onto an old chair, then one corner of the sofa, then the bed, then under the covers, and then on the pillow. Go ahead and decide now what your pup is going to be allowed on, and be consistent. You can always go from strict to lenient, but going from lenient to strict is not going to be easy. If she gets onto forbidden furniture, simply take her off and make sure you spend a lot of time on the floor with her. Also make sure she has some cuddly dog beds near where you will be sitting or sleeping. Frenchies do like their creature comforts.

## Leash Walking

Frenchies are nudists by nature. They consider themselves free spirits unencumbered by collars, harnesses, or leashes. Like you, though, they have to make concessions to civilization, and that means accepting these bare necessities. Many people find a harness is easier to walk a Frenchie on than a collar because it has less chance of being pulled over the head. If you do use a collar, choose a buckle or martingale collar. A slip, or choke, collar is fine to use while walking in public, but you must never forget and leave it on when she is loose. Your leash should be nylon or leather, never chain, because chain is difficult to handle and tends to smack your Frenchie in the face.

The first time you put a leash or collar onto your Frenchie pup, she may roll around and bite at it. Distract her with lots of treats or even a game. Have her wear it for only a short time, and remove it while she is being good. Repeat several times a day until she associates a collar or harness with good times.

Now for the leash. Do not try to lead her anywhere with it. She is a Frenchie, and she has her pride. Let her proudly lead you around the house and yard. If she appears glued in place, pick her up and move her to another place, or entice her to take a few steps by luring her

with a treat. Gradually lure her more and more. Require that she take a few steps along with you before she gets the treats . . . then a few more steps. Gradually, she will figure out that walking alongside you turns you into a human snack machine, and just about any Frenchie can be led by her stomach.

## FRENCHIE PEDIATRICS

Your Frenchie baby needs special care to grow up healthy. Start with a veterinary exam within a day of bringing her home. Your veterinarian is your best source of individualized health care, but you should be aware of the basics.

### Puppy Food

Feeding a Frenchie puppy can be daunting. She will eat just about anything. So you must make sure that what you put into her bowl is nutritious. Now is not the time to save money by buying the pressed husks and guts that pass for generic dog food. Feed a high-quality food made especially for puppies.

Your young puppy should be fed four times a day. Let her eat as much as she wants in about 15 minutes, then pick up the bowl. From about four to six months of age, you can feed her either three or four times a day. From six to nine months of age, feed three times a day, and then gradually cut down to twice a day by the time she is 12 months old. You can add snacks, but do not let her get fat. If you see her packing on

the baby fat, cut down the amount she eats per meal.

## Vaccinations

Only a few years ago, vaccinations were a nonissue. "The more the better" was the mantra. Now veterinarians have adopted a more individualized approach to vaccination. The basic concepts of puppy vaccination remain the same, however. Without well-timed vaccinations, your Frenchie can be vulnerable to deadly communicable diseases.

Your pup received her early immunity through her dam's colostrum during the first few days of nursing. As long as your pup still has that immunity, any vaccinations you give her will not provide sufficient immunity. However, after several weeks, that immunity begins to decrease. As her immunity falls, both the chance of a vaccination being effective and the chance of getting a communicable disease rise. The problem is that immunity diminishes at different times in different dogs. So starting at around six weeks of age, a series of vaccinations are given in order to catch the time when they will be effective while leaving as little unprotected time as possible. During this time of uncertainty, do not take your pup to places where unvaccinated dogs may congregate. Some deadly viruses, such as parvovirus, can remain in the soil for six months after an infected dog has shed virus in his feces there.

Core and noncore: This does not mean you must load up on every vaccine available. Vaccinations are divided into core vaccines, which are advisable for all dogs, and noncore vaccines, which are advisable only for some dogs. Core vaccines are those for rabies, dis-

temper, parvovirus, and adenovirus (using the CAV-2 vaccine, not the CAV-1, which can cause adverse reactions and is still sold by some feed stores). Noncore vaccines include those for leptospirosis, corona virus, tracheobronchitis, and Lyme disease. Your veterinarian can advise you if your dog's lifestyle and environment put her at risk for these diseases. Remember, more is not better!

A sample core vaccination protocol for puppies suggests giving a three-injection series at least two weeks apart, with each injection containing distemper (or measles for the first injection), parvovirus, adenovirus 2 (CAV-2), and possibly parainfluenza (CPIV). The series should not end before 12 weeks of age. A

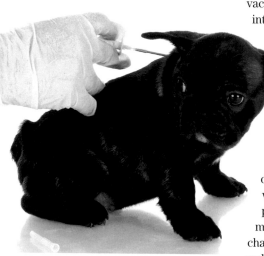

vaccinated, their dog probably never comes into contact with the infectious agents. No controlled study has ever supported the effectiveness of nosodes. Vaccinations are not without a downside, but they are essential components of your dog's healthy future. Do not take chances.

## Deworming

Your pup should have been checked and dewormed if necessary before coming home with you. Most pups have worms at some point because some types of worms lie dormant and protected in the dam until hormonal changes caused by her pregnancy activate them and enable them to infect her puppies. Your pup can also pick up worms from the ground in places where dogs congregate. The best prevention at home is to clean up feces immediately. Some heartworm preventives also prevent many types of worms. Get your pup regular fecal checks for worms, but do not deworm your pup unnecessarily. Avoid over-the-counter worm medications, which are neither as safe nor effective as those available from your veterinarian.

If you see small, flat, white segments in your dog's stool, she may have tapeworms. Tapeworms are acquired when your pup eats a flea, so the best prevention is flea prevention. Tapeworms require special medication to get rid of them.

## Heartworm Prevention

Heartworms can kill your dog. They are carried by mosquitoes. If there is any chance of a single mosquito biting your Frenchie, she needs to be on heartworm-preventive medication.

booster is given one year later, and then boosters are given every three years. Rabies should be given at 16 weeks of age, with boosters at one- to three-year intervals according to local law.

How frequently boosters should be given is currently under scrutiny. Evidence exists that many vaccinations are still imparting immunity for as long as seven years! Some owners elect to test their dogs' blood titers to various diseases to see if a booster is needed. A high titer generally indicates protection, but a low titer does not mean the dog is not protected.

Some proponents of natural rearing condemn vaccinations and refuse to use them. They use homeopathic nosodes instead and point to the fact that their dogs do not get sick as proof that they work. However, their good fortune is probably the result of herd immunity. In other words, as long as most other dogs are

Ask your veterinarian when she should begin taking the medication, as it may vary according to your location. Dogs over six months of age should be checked for heartworms with a simple blood test before beginning heartworm prevention. The once-a-month preventive is safe, convenient, and effective. Treatment is available for heartworms. However, preventing them is far cheaper, easier, and safer.

## Spaying and Neutering

Something about getting a purebred puppy turns on a stupid center in many people's brain. They look upon this 12-week-old baby and start to imagine breeding her, making wheelbarrows of money, and calling themselves breeders. Their brains blot out the reality of the inconvenience of having an intact adult, the dangers of breeding, the work involved in caring for puppies, the expense incurred in raising them, the difficulty of finding good homes, and the lifelong responsibility breeding entails. Pay attention.

**Estrus:** An intact (unspayed) female comes into estrus twice a year, usually beginning at around eight months of age. Each heat period lasts for about three weeks, during which she will have a bloody discharge that will ruin your furnishings or necessitate her being crated for three weeks or wearing little britches (which you will forget to remove when you let her out to potty and will then have a real mess on your hands). Her scent, which she will advertise by urinating as much as possible, will advertise your home as a roadside brothel. You may have lots of uninvited canine Don Juans camping at

your door. If you have an intact male of your own, he will drive you insane with his relentless panting, whining, shaking, and clawing. It will be the longest three weeks of your life.

Birth problems: The Frenchie's wide head and comparatively narrow pelvis makes natural birth sometimes impossible. A planned caesarean section is comparatively safe (although anesthetizing a Frenchie is always a concern). Unfortunately, most first-time breeders wait until the dam is in trouble, when only an emergency caesarean section can save her and the pups. Surgery under these circumstances is expensive and risky. The dam may also develop a host of postwhelping problems, some of which will require you to bottle-feed puppies. Once the pups are whelped, you will need to feed and clean up after them tirelessly.

How would you find homes for the pups? Do you trust that the people who answer your advertisements will give your pup a home as good as yours? Will you commit to being responsible for that pup's well-being for the rest of her life? Will you take every puppy back if their new owners should tire of them or otherwise not be able to keep them? That could add up to a houseful of Frenchies!

Good Frenchie breeders make these commitments and more. They screen for hereditary defects, prove their dogs in some form of competition, educate themselves, and stand by their puppies for a lifetime. They often require that buyers neuter or spay their dogs because they know too well the problems dog breeding can create. They also recognize the health advantages that go along with spaying and neutering.

Intact females are at increased risk of developing breast cancer and pyometra, a potentially fatal infection of the uterus. In fact, Frenchies seem to be more prone to pyometra compared with some breeds. Spaying negates the possibility of pyometra, and spaying before the first season significantly reduces the chance of breast cancer. Intact males are more likely to roam or fight and to develop testicular cancer and prostatitis. The major drawbacks are that spaying and neutering each require surgery and anesthesia, that many spayed and neutered dogs gain weight, and that some spayed females develop urinary incontinence. Talk to your veterinarian and breeder about the pros and cons.

# For Goodness Sake

Even clowns need to have some lessons in daily manners. He's sure to add his own comedic twist to everything you teach him, but that is the joy of training a Frenchie!

# POSITIVELY GOOD!

If the prospect of forcing your Frenchie into obeying upsets you, good—that is not how things are done these days. The old push and jerk school of dog training is out of style, and it should be. It was no fun for human or dog, and it did not work very well. Dogs were labeled stubborn or stupid because they did not immediately succumb to pressure. French Bulldogs were foremost among the breeds that were more likely to dig in their heels and rebel. Their bully heritage came to the surface and reminded all that you cannot out-tough a bull breed.

**A little psychology** should come into play. By using the same methods used to train performing animals, now anybody can train a dog, even a Frenchie, with ease and fun. Nobody, human or canine, likes to be forced to do something. When they can avoid it, they will. When they cannot, they will do the bare minimum. However, everybody likes to be rewarded. You do not work for free, so why should your dog? When you are rewarded enough, you will go out of your way to do even more than what is asked. New training methods focus on fun, food, and positive associations. They produce happy, well-trained dogs that are eager to learn more.

**What about punishment?** Punishment is not a good way to teach a dog to do anything. About the only thing it is good for is to teach a dog to do nothing. If you want a dog that does nothing, you should get a stuffed toy dog!

**A good place:** Before you start, find a quiet place away from distractions. Only when your dog learns a skill very well should you gradually start practicing it in other places. Do not try to train your dog if he is tired, hot, or has just eaten. You want him peppy and hungry for your fun and treats. Do not train your dog if you are impatient or mad. You will not be able to hide your frustration, and your dog will be uneasy. Losing your cool one time can undo days of proper training. Keep your training sessions short—very short. Dogs learn best in 10- to 15-minute sessions. Always quit while he is still having fun and doing something he can do well. You can train him several times a day if you want.

**Collar:** In the old days, your dog had to wear a choke, or slip, collar for training. That occurred because training traditionally involved correcting the dog with a quick snap and release. It was not supposed to choke him, but it was supposed to be startling. With positive methods, you can use such a collar, but you are

Be sure to click as soon as you can when your dog does what you want. Doing so marks the event and tells the dog, "Yes, that's it!" Then reward as soon as you can after the click. Do not forget the praise! Does that mean you have to click to your dog forever? No! You click to tell the dog that he has done the right thing only as he is learning something. After you are sure he knows how to do something, you quit giving him the click. Still, remember to give him praise and rewards!

No dog learns to do something perfectly at first. You have to teach him gradually, shaping his behavior closer and closer to what you want. By following the clicker sound with a reward, your dog tries to repeat what he did to get the click. Now pretend to teach your Frenchie, who we have imaginatively named "Frenchie," how to sit as an example of how to click a trick.

just as well off using a buckle collar. You will not be tugging on it. You will want a 6-foot (2 m) leash (not chain!) and maybe a 20-foot (6 m) light line. Now you are ready!

## THE CLICK IS THE TRICK

Your Frenchie does not understand people rules or language. He hears a constant stream of words, few of which are directed to him. So he learns to tune out most of them. If you really want your dog to pay attention, use a sound he does not normally hear. Serious dog trainers use a clicker, an inexpensive device available at pet stores that makes a click sound when pressed. The clicker is used to signal "Good!" and is always followed by a reward. If you do not have a clicker, you can make a distinctive click sound yourself, although it does not seem to be quite as effective.

## Click to Sit

The old way of teaching the *sit* was to pull up on your dog's collar and push down on his rear as you said, *"Sit."* It was like holding an inflated balloon under water—as soon as you removed your hand, it would pop back up. Clicking this first trick takes a little longer initially, but it lays the groundwork for superfast learning in the long run. First, review these clicker basics:

- Always train in gradual steps. Give rewards for getting closer and closer to the final trick.
- Give a click instantly when your dog does what you want. The faster you click, the easier your dog will figure out what you like.
- Give a reward as soon as you can after the click.

- Do not forget to praise and pet your dog as part of the reward!
- Say your dog's name just before you give the command cue word so he knows the next word you babble is directed at him.
- Give the command cue just before you get the dog to do the behavior, not during or after it.
- Just say a cue word once. Repeating it over and over will not help your dog learn it.
- Once your dog has learned the completed trick and is doing it consistently, you do not have to click your approval anymore. However, you still need to praise and reward him.

You will need a way to make a click sound and many, many tiny treats, such as tiny bits of hot dog. You could go to a quiet room and wait for Frenchie to sit on his own, then click and reward him. That might take a while. So you could wait for him to bend his knees and then click and reward, reinforcing him for squatting just a bit. Once he has learned to do that, you could wait until he squats a bit more before clicking, until finally, going in gradual steps, you would actually require him to sit before you click and reward. This method, too, can be time-consuming. So you can hasten the process by luring him into position. With his rear in a corner so he cannot back up, take your treat and hold it just above and behind his nose, so he has to bend his rear legs to look up at it. Click and reward. Repeat several times, then move the treat further back so Frenchie has to bend his legs more. Keep on until he has to sit.

Only when he is sitting reliably to the treat lure do you introduce a cue word, "Frenchie,

*Sit.*" Gradually fade out use of the treat lure, using just your hand at first, and then nothing. Be sure to continue giving it as his final reward, though. Congratulations! You have taught your Frenchie to sit without jerking on his collar or pushing on his rear. He probably thinks this is pretty fun. He probably would like to learn some other ways to con you out of some good treats. Fortunately, you have some ideas.

## Click to Down

In the old days, you would teach Frenchie to lie down by wrestling his front legs to the ground. Any self-respecting Frenchie would resist. There is an easier way.

With Frenchie sitting or standing, use your treat to lure his nose down and forward. You may have to prevent him from walking forward by gently restraining him with your other hand. Click and reward for just putting his nose down and forward a bit, then for reaching to

39

the ground, then for lowering his elbows a bit, and then for lying all the way down. Once he is doing that, click and reward for doing it only when you give the cue, "Frenchie, *Down!*" Then try it on different surfaces. Once again, you have taught your dog to do something useful without jerking or wrestling.

## Click to Stay

Normally when you teach your dog *sit* or *down*, he should stay in position until you give a click, which is his release signal. So once your dog knows *sit* or *down*, wait a few seconds after he is in position before clicking and rewarding. Tell him, *"Stay."* (This command does not use his name in front of it, because some dogs tend to jump up when they hear their name.) Gradually lengthen the time he must stay before getting the click and reward.

You can step out just in front of him to face him, then pivot back in place before clicking and rewarding. Gradually step a little farther and farther away, and return to him by circling behind. Click and reward. Go a little farther away, or stay a little longer time. Remember, it is better for him to succeed than to fail, so do not push his limits. If he does get up, simply put him back in position and have him stay a shorter time.

## Click to Heel

In the old days, you trained dogs to heel by letting them forge ahead and then jerking them back into position. This taught the dog to keep an eye on you because you were an unpredictable menace on a leash. To watch you better, the dog tended to lag behind you. Heeling was not a happy affair.

To train with a clicker, you do not even need a leash, although it does help. Your aim is to have your dog walk abreast of your left leg. If your dog is not leash trained, place him on a leash and just walk with him. Click and reward when he is by your side. Show him a treat, and encourage him to walk a few feet with you for it. Click and reward. Work up to slightly longer distances. If he balks or fights the lead, just stop or go in a different direction. You can perfect his position if you want a good heeling dog by rewarding only when he is by your left leg. Again, shape him gradually to get to that point. Once there, introduce the cue, "Frenchie, *Heel!*"

Heeling in the backyard is one thing. Heeling down the sidewalk is another. If he insists on pulling you down the sidewalk he may see something he wants more than your treat. In that case, turn away from what he wants and tell him to heel. Once he does so, click and reward him by saying "OK" and letting him go investigate. Gradually require him to walk a few steps toward the object without pulling before giving him his click and OK. Sometimes heeling is a compromise.

## Click to Come

Coming when called is not a compromise. Your dog already knows how to come when he sees you setting down his dinner. Your job is to make him want to come that eagerly every time you call him. You do this by rewarding him when he comes to you. Keep some treats—and your clicker—in your pocket, and do not be stingy with them when he comes. Even if he has been up to mischief, be sure not to reprimand him when he comes. Frenchies are smart enough to figure out they will be better off staying away next time.

If you have a helper, you can play a game that will get your Frenchie really running to you. In an enclosed area, such as a hallway, have your friend hold your pup while you show him a treat or toy. Back away, enticing him until he is struggling to get to you. Then call out, "Frenchie, *Come!*" and turn and run away from him just as your friend releases him. As he gets to you, click and give him the treat. Make a game out of running faster and farther from him. Always quit while he still wants to play more.

Once your Frenchie learns the basics of clicker training, you will quickly run through the basic commands. Use your imagination. Teach your dog to shake, roll over, speak, play dead, ride a skateboard, count, jump through a

hoop, or anything you can imagine. Just use the same basic shape, click, and reward concept.

## FRENCH LANGUAGE 101

Do you speak Frenchie? Do not expect your dog to learn your human language without making an effort to learn his. Here is a start for your Frenchie-to-human translation book:

- When your Frenchie crouches low to the ground, tucking and wagging his tail (or butt) while holding his ears down and trying to lick

your face, he is saying, "Please don't be mad at me! I want you to love me!"

- When he tucks his tail (what there is of it), stands still, holds his ears back, yawns, or licks his lips repeatedly, he is saying, "I'm a little nervous."
- When he rolls on his back with his tongue lolling out, maybe grunting and groaning, he is saying, "Life is good."
- When he nudges you with his muzzle or places a paw onto you, he is saying, "Pay attention to me!"
- When he does a wet dog shake for no apparent reason, he is saying, "Whew, glad that's over!"
- When he rests both front legs on the ground while leaving his rear in the air, he is saying, "Let's play!"
- When he stands tall and puts his head over another dog's back, he is saying, "I'm the boss."
- When he makes a soft growling-like sound while playing, he is not growling, he is doing the doggy laugh.

Remember, your Frenchie's world is different than yours. He pays more attention to your body language than to your words. He smells things you cannot imagine and hears better too. He sees better at night, but his color vision and acuity are not as good as yours. When you have a failure to communicate, think about whether it is really a failure to perceive the world the same way.

## BAD BULLY!

When you ask a member of another species to coexist in your world according to your rules that often make no sense, misunderstandings can happen. Your rules against digging up the flowers, barking at the cat, and chewing on your shoes seem pretty arbitrary to a dog. Your dog's concerns about being left alone, greeting strangers, or coping with thunderstorms seem pretty overblown to you. In the old days owners tried to reason with their dogs with punishment and then thought the dogs were stubborn because the situation usually got worse. Behavior problems are the number one killer of dogs,

## House Soiling

If an adult soils the house, especially if the dog was previously housetrained, a veterinary exam is warranted to consider the following medical problems:

✔ Spayed females may dribble urine, especially when sleeping. Drug therapies can often satisfactorily treat this.

✔ Older dogs may not have the bladder control they once had. Consider a doggy door or litter box.

✔ Older dogs may have cognitive dysfunction. Drug therapy may help.

✔ Females, especially, may have urinary tract infections. Suspect this if she urinates small amounts frequently.

✔ Older dogs, especially, may have diabetes or kidney disease that causes increased thirst and urination. They need veterinary treatment.

✔ Intact males may be marking. Castration may help (but often does not once the habit is established).

✔ Intact females may be coming into estrus (heat). Spaying should help.

Also consider behavioral problems:

✔ Young females, especially, tend to urinate in submission upon greetings. Greet them calmly, outside if possible, and do not do anything to make them more submissive.

✔ Dogs of any age may be suffering from separation anxiety.

ior modification and, sometimes, drug therapy. Although therapies vary according to problems, they all stress one concept: Punishment never teaches your dog anything except to fear you.

Dogs have a limited capacity to understand cause and effect over an extended time period. That means if you come home and your dog has ripped up your house, no matter how much pointing and nose rubbing and yelling you do, the only thing that will register with him is that you may be a homicidal maniac. He may start to relate your return home with another of your crazed outbursts. However, he will not associate it with digging up the carpet three hours ago. Then why does he look so guilty? He can learn to predict that when you come home you'll go crazy, so he will become increasingly anxious when you are due home. He can associate "house in shambles" with "owner having fit," so he may start to act submissively when the

mainly because people give up on their dogs when they cannot cope with the dogs' behavior.

There is hope. Veterinary behaviorists specialize in treating such problems, using behav-

house is messed up, even when he did not make the mess himself. This home destruction is one of the most common, and misunderstood, of all dog behavior problems. Therefore, let us start with it.

## Home Destruction

What could turn a nice, nondestructive dog into a one-dog demolition team when you leave the house? If you think it is spite, you are back in the dark ages and you will never fix the problem.

**Anxiety:** When an adult Frenchie destroys your home while you are away, he is probably not trying to destroy anything but, instead, trying to cope with his anxiety at being left alone.

Dogs are not loners. Domestic dogs become extremely dependent on you as their surrogate pack leader. If a wild dog in a pack were separated from the pack, he would do whatever he could to be reunited. That is why many dogs that destroy when left alone center their destruction around doors, windows, and other escape routes. In their minds, that is the best way to find you. They may dig, chew, bark, and howl. They may pace, pant, tremble, salivate, urinate, and defecate out of anxiety. If you lock the dog in a crate, he may be no better, although the digging, drooling, urinating, and defecating will be confined to the crate. Some dogs break teeth in their efforts to escape the crate. Spiting you is the last thing on your dog's

mind. He is suffering from separation anxiety. It will not fix itself, and punishment definitely will not help.

Fixing this problem will take time and effort. Downplay your departures and returns. Ignore the dog for 30 minutes before leaving. If you give him attention, do it only when he is not trying to solicit attention from you. Reward him for being calm. Teach him to ignore your predeparture cues, such as putting on your shoes or picking up the keys, by doing that randomly throughout the day without going anywhere. Teach him instead a safety signal, such as an air freshener spray, that will mean to him you are coming right back. Spray the spray, then leave for 30 seconds and return. This signal is his assurance that you will be right back. However, do not use it early in training if you plan to be gone all day. Gradually build up the time, never allowing the dog to be alone long enough to get stressed. Repeat this exercise about 10 times a day. When you return, ignore the dog until he is calm, and then reward him for doing a simple trick. You may need to add an antianxiety drug (prescribed by a veterinary behaviorist) to your behavior modification program at first. Dog-appeasing pheromones and anxiety wraps may also be beneficial.

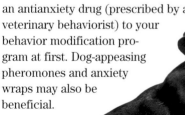

Although separation anxiety is the most common cause of home destruction, it is not the only one. Puppies, especially, are like French bulls in a china shop, leaving a trail of destruction. Confine them to a safe place. Give them a special toy, preferably an interactive one that takes the dogs lots of time to extract treats from. Other dogs may pull down curtains because they see something they want to chase outside the window. They may dig in an effort to hide from something, such as a thunderstorm, that scares them. Sometimes videotaping the dog while you are gone can tell you the cause.

Fears and phobias: Like us, dogs can have illogical fears. High on the list are loud noises, like thunder or firecrackers. These phobias can be difficult to deal with because once you realize the dog has a problem, it is usually well-ingrained. You can play tapes of thunder

**45**

while you reward your dog for being relaxed and for doing some tricks. Gradually increase the volume. Tapes do not always help. A veterinary behaviorist can also prescribe antianxiety drugs to give during training or storms, which may help if given quickly enough. Dog-appeasing pheromones and antianxiety wraps may help a little.

Many dogs are also afraid of other dogs or of strange people. The best cure is prevention, with lots of socialization as a young pup. As an adult, the best treatment is to expose the dog to other dogs or strangers gradually. Reward your dog for doing a trick in sight of them. Gradually move closer. The people or dogs should ignore your dog. Eventually, you should be able to walk your dog on leash alongside another dog and to let your dog sniff a strange person and accept a treat from that person.

Never overwhelm a dog with what it is afraid of; doing so only makes matters worse. Always go in slow, gradual steps, teaching the dog to be confident at one level before moving to the next.

## Barking

Frenchies are not bad barkers. Occasionally, though, one will be a little too proud of his voice. Is he barking at something or because he is bored or lonely? If he barks in his crate try moving the crate to a more populated area or next to your bed at night. If he is barking in a pen outside, bring him into the yard or house where he should be living as part of the family. If he is barking out of excitement, try to learn what cues set him off, and intercept by rewarding him for doing a trick or remaining quiet. Use your clicker-training concept to reward him for gradually longer and longer periods of quiet.

## Digging

All dogs dig. Frenchies are not bad offenders in this area, though. However, you can direct your Frenchie's digging to his own area by making him a little sandbox. Seed it with toys and treasures to encourage digging there. If he digs elsewhere, take him to his area.

## Stool Eating

Few things can appall dog owners as much as the sight of their beloved dog they were just kissing snacking on dog doo-doo. Technically called coprophagia, it is not uncommon in dogs, especially puppies. Despite several studies and lots of theories, nobody knows why they do it. It has been blamed on boredom, stress, hunger, poor nutrition, and excessively rich nutrition, but no one theory holds up. The best cure is getting to the stools before your dog does. You can also buy food additives available at pet supply stores that will make the feces taste somehow even worse than plain, untreated dog feces.

Remember, the only perfectly behaved dog is a stuffed toy dog. However, they are not nearly as much fun as your sometimes less-than-perfect Frenchie.

# Bull Games

From backyard games to road trips, dog shows to therapy visits, your Frenchie will tackle each new challenge with the gusto only a Frenchie can manage. There is a world of adventure awaiting you and your Frenchie—so what are you waiting for?

## BULLY BEAUTIES

Of course your Frenchie is beautiful—in an elfin sort of way. If she also conforms closely to the French Bulldog breed standard, she may have the makings of a show dog.

Deciding if a dog is show quality can be tough for the uninitiated, so start with your breeders. If they show their dogs they can tell you if your dog has show potential. Study the breed standard (see pages 60–61) and try to compare your dog objectively. No dog is perfect, so do not despair if things do not seem to match in every regard. However, if nothing matches, maybe your dog was not meant to be a show star. One more thing, if your dog is a male, he must have two normally descended testicles to be shown. In fact, dogs cannot compete in most AKC conformation classes if they are spayed or neutered.

Often a local kennel club, which you can locate through the AKC, will sponsor conformation classes. Here your Frenchie will learn how to strut around the ring, pose, and turn on the charm. You can practice posing your dog at home by placing her front legs parallel to each other and perpendicular to the ground and her rear legs also parallel to one another with the hocks (the area from the rear ankle to the foot) perpendicular to the ground. Practice having her trot alertly in a straight line. More important than getting everything perfect is doing it all with a happy attitude. You help her keep this merry outlook with the liberal handouts of treats.

At a show, a judge will evaluate your Frenchie in regard to type—that is, how well she exemplifies the areas of the standard that define a Frenchie as a Frenchie. These areas

include head shape, ear shape, and overall proportions. She will also be evaluated on soundness, her ability to walk or trot in as efficient a manner as possible. Finally, she will be evaluated on temperament, checking that she is not shy, aggressive, or sulking. If she ranks high in comparison with her competition, she may win points toward her championship. Points are awarded to the top dog of either sex that is not already a champion. From one to five points can be won at each show according to the number of dogs defeated. To become an AKC champion, she needs to win 15 points, including twice winning at least three points at once. If she is judged the best nonchampion of her sex, she will also compete for the best Frenchie, or Best of Breed. That winner then goes on to compete in the Non-Sporting group, the winner of which then competes with the six other group winners for Best in Show.

## Rally O!

Rally obedience is a less regimented style of obedience in which you and your dog follow a course along which various signs tell you what to do next. Directions include things such as *"Sit," "Step to the side," "Spiral,"* and *"Jump."* Three levels are offered: novice, advanced, and excellent. You can praise and talk to your dog throughout. The dog's willingness and enjoyment are more important than is precision.

Even if you leave the show ribbonless, you will have lots of company. Just do not let your Frenchie know, and make sure you enjoy the day for what it should be: a fun outing with your dog where you can meet other Frenchie folk.

## MIND GAMES

Your Frenchie need not be a canine Einstein to breeze through the AKC Canine Good Citizenship test and even earn an AKC obedience title. When competing, bring her buckle or slip collar, brush or comb, and proof of rabies vaccination.

**French citizenship:** The Canine Good Citizen (CGC) certificate attests that your dog is well-behaved in public. To show what a good citizen she is, she will have to:

- Accept a friendly stranger without acting shy or resentful or breaking position to approach; sitting politely for petting and allowing the stranger to examine her ears, feet, and coat and to brush her.

- Walk politely on a loose leash, turning and stopping with you, walking through a group of at least three other people without jumping on them, pulling, or acting overly exuberant, shy, or resentful. She need not be perfectly aligned with you, but she should not be pulling.
- Sit and lie down on command (you can gently guide her into position) and then stay as you walk 20 feet (60 m) away and back.
- Stay and then come to you when called from 10 feet (30 m) away.
- Behave politely to another dog and handler team, showing only casual interest in them.
- React calmly to distractions such as a dropped chair or passing jogger without panicking, barking, or acting aggressively.
- Remain calm when held by a stranger while you are out of sight for three minutes.
- Refrain from eliminating, growling, snapping, biting, or attempting to attack a person or dog throughout the evaluation.

All the tests are done on lead; a long line is provided for the stay and recall exercises. If your Frenchie passes, she will receive a Canine Good Citizen certificate from the AKC.

The AKC also offers an advanced version, the AKC Community Canine, with ten slightly more challenging exercises. To get started toward either title, visit the AKC Community Canine page on *www.akc.org*.

**The French academy:** Is your Frenchie gifted? Prove it! At AKC obedience trials, your Frenchie's obedience will be evaluated against a perfect performance in both individual and group exercises in a series of successively more challenging routines. At the novice level, heeling is done both on and off lead, with the dog

staying in position through right, left, and about turns and sitting each time you stop. A figure eight around two people is also done, but only on lead. Then follows a stand for exam off lead, where the judge touches your dog while you stand several feet away, a recall to you after the dog has stayed on the other side of the ring, and a group *sit-stay* for one minute and *down-stay* for three minutes. If your dog passes this test three times, she is officially recorded as a Companion Dog.

Not quite ready? Try Beginner's Novice, in which all exercises are on leash and there's no group *stay*.

## French Toasts of the Town

✔ The top AKC show French Bulldog of all time: Ch. Ralanda Ami Francine, who won an amazing 55 Best in Shows.

✔ The top French Bulldog Club of America National Specialty winner: Ch. Bouquet Nouvelle Ami, who won it in 1953, 1954, 1956, and 1957. Jo-Jo was Francine's grandsire and once held the record for most male Best in Show wins (30). He earned eight consecutive Best of Breed wins at Westminster.

✔ The top obedience Frenchie of all time: OTCH Marianette Joyeuse Cuvée Sylvain, UDX2, CGC. Joy is the only Frenchie to ever earn the obedience trial champion (OTCH) title. Along the way, Joy won five High in Trial Awards, five High Combined Scores (open plus utility at the same trial), and a perfect score of 200 in utility. Joy followed in the pawprints of the first UDX Frenchie, her housemate Fishers Champagne Sylvain, UDX, CGC.

✔ To date, four Frenchies have earned the agility champion (MACH) title. One, MACH3 Amron's Rewriting The Rules (AKA Scribbles), has earned the required points three times over!

✔ The most titled Frenchie in history is Daulokke's Une Valliant Grosse Silver (AKA Soren), who counts among his 93 titles a MACH2, PACH4, CD, and ROM.

✔ In 2010, Dub'L-J Solow Noire Magie O'Crosstrack TD became the first Frenchie to earn a Tracking Dog title.

✔ Six Frenchies hold flyball titles from the North Amercian Flyball Association. The highest scoring flyball Frenchie is Libellule Beautiful Lady (AKA Jbilee), who has earned the coveted ONYX title.

More advanced open classes include jumping and retrieving, and they lead to the Companion Dog Excellent title. These are followed by utility classes that include directed jumping, hand signals, and scent discrimination leading to the Utility Dog title. Yet higher titles are the Utility Dog Excellent and the Obedience Trial Champion.

Your success rate will be much higher if you join a training class where you can practice together and get training tips. Still, do not expect to pass every trial. At first you will make mistakes and your dog will make mistakes. Do not dwell on failures, but use them as fodder for a great tale at your next class meeting. After all, passing makes for boring stories. However, with a Frenchie's imagination, every failure is an adventure worth recounting!

## More Frenchie Frolics

Frenchies can have a blast participating in AKC Coursing Ability Tests where they chase a plastic bag around a 200 yard course. While some Frenchies look at you like you must be insane expecting them to chase anything not edible, others let their inner wolf take over and rocket around the field. Frenchies should only run in cool weather, and only if they have no breathing difficulties.  The AKC offers titles based on how many times a dog has a qualify-

ing run; several Frenchies have earned the CA title, which requires three passes, and one has earned the CAX title, which requires 25 passes.

Frenchies can also tap into their inner hunter at Barn Hunt tests, where they find and mark hidden rats in a barn-like setting. The rat is safely ensconced in a PVC tube hidden among a maze of hay bales. Higher levels require finding more rats. This is a new sport, but already several Frenchies have earned lower level titles.

French Bulldogs can also participate in tracking, in which they follow a scent trail; flyball, in which they are part of a relay team where they run a short distance, jump some small jumps on the way, grab a ball and run back; canine freestyle, where they essentially dance with you to music; and nosework, where they use their nose to find a hidden scent.

Leap frogs: OK, so Frenchies do not exactly exemplify the agile gymnast's physique. However, you know they can do some amazing feats of agility with their rotund bodies. They can jump high enough to steal food, tunnel under the sofa to retrieve an errant piece of kibble, and climb onto any furniture. If they can do that, they have the basic skills to compete in agility. Of course, they will need to learn to do each obstacle in the order you tell them and to do them with some precision.

Agility is basically an obstacle course for dogs. The standard course obstacles include various jumps, open and closed tunnels, weave poles, a pause table, a teeter, a tall A-frame, and an elevated balance beam (do not worry—it is plenty wide for your wide Frenchie). The jumps can be single bars, double bars, broad, solid, and even a tire. An alternative course type, called jumpers with weaves (JWW), just uses the jumps, tunnels, and weaves. If the jumps seem too high for your dog, you can elect to compete in the Preferred class, which has lower jump heights. In fact, you should check with your veterinarian beforehand to make sure your Frenchie does not have back or joint problems that could be aggravated by jumping. All of the classes have novice, open, and excellent levels with progressively harder courses and shorter times. Your job is to guide your dog from obstacle to obstacle off lead within a certain time limit. Your dog must pass at each level three times to earn each agility title.

Do not stop there! The world of canine competition has something for everyone! How about freestyle, where dogs and their people dance to music, or tracking, where dogs follow a scent trail? Remember, you can also just enjoy your dog in noncompetitive activities.

## FUN WITH FRENCHIES

Competitions are fun. However, every Frenchie owner knows the real joys of living with a Frenchie are the everyday adventures, whether quick trips to the park, long drives across country, or manic games at home.

### Games

One of the best parts of having any dog, especially a French Bulldog, is the excuse to act like a kid and play all sorts of games. Here are a few ideas to get you started.

Fetch: Most dogs like to chase balls, and Frenchies are no exception. The problem is that they do not always bring them back. Since Frenchies are easy to bribe with food, you can teach your dog that you will trade a treat for the ball. You may have to start in a confined space so she can get the idea. Make absolutely sure your Frenchie cannot inhale the ball; balls can get stuck in a dog's windpipe, causing asphyxiation. In fact, balls can get stuck in the Frenchie's mouth.

Treasure hunt: Let your Frenchie see you hide small dog biscuits around the house or yard. Then take her out of sight for a few minutes before letting her return to find as many as she can. This is a great memory-building exercise.

On the trail: Frenchies may not be known for their sense of smell, but it is still amazing

## Little Dog Lost

It can happen to even the most conscientious and careful of owners. The unexpected occurs, and your dog is missing. Most lost dogs are found, but the sooner you organize, the better your chances.

✔ Begin your search by going to the most likely place your dog has gone, which is usually some place she's been before; and the most dangerous place she could go, which is usually a road.

✔ When calling, leave quiet periods. Dogs tend to be quiet when they hear you, and noisy when they don't.

✔ If you're away from home, maintain a base where you last saw your dog. Camp, leave your car with a door open, or leave her crate with blankets or some of your used clothing.

✔ Call, visit, or befriend local veterinarians, animal control officers, and shelters.

✔ Contact organizers of any local events such as trial riding, hiking, or off-roading.

✔ Make large posters that state in large red letters "REWARD" and include a clear photo of your Frenchie and your phone number in large print. Place them at eye level at intersections, along sidewalks, and anywhere with traffic.

✔ Make fliers or business cards to hand out and post at post offices, markets, laundromats, and popular locations.

✔ Give fliers to the police, delivery people, school bus drivers, and refuse collectors.

✔ Contact local kennel clubs and training groups to see if anyone can help search.

✔ Take out a classified ad in the newspaper and see if radio stations will mention it.

✔ Post on Craigslist, Facebook, and Twitter, or on any local or breed-oriented Internet groups.

✔ Contact your microchip company. They may have additional lost pet services–or a report!

✔ Check the Center for Lost Pets, Flealess Market's Lost Pets International, Missing Pet Network, Missing Pets, and Fido Finder online sites.

✔ Find Toto and Pet Amber Alert and send automated phone calls in minutes to local pet-related businesses and to neighbors.

✔ Help Me Find My Pet e-mails local pet-related businesses as well as people who have signed up to receive alerts within a 25 mile (40 km) radius.

✔ Give lost Pet Cards and Pet Harbor mail postcards with your dog's photo to everyone in your area within a day.

✔ Most important: Act fast, and don't give up!

compared to yours. You can encourage her to use it by challenging her to follow your scent trail. Start by walking a short distance and dropping food treats every step. Gradually increase the distance between food drops, praising your Frenchie each time she finds a treat. Eventually she will realize that if she follows your scent trail, it will lead to a pot of gold—or at least, treats—at the end. Of course, be careful each trail is laid in a fresh area not crossed by your scent.

## Adventures

Your Frenchie will enjoy outdoor adventures, but it's up to you to make her do so in moderation. Do not expect her to be your running companion. Her physique is built for strength, not speed or running stamina. She will enjoy hiking, but she is not one to tackle the Appalachian Trail or any rough going. Steep hills are difficult for Frenchies. Short hikes in a safe area, away from cliffs, hills, caves, and wild animals, will be exciting for her and let her play wild dog as she explores.

This is not a dog for warm-weather activities. Her physique is a recipe for overheating. Her chunky body, with a lot of mass compared with its surface area, holds in heat more than a slender body would. Her short nose and sometimes compressed air intake area makes it difficult for her to breathe and cool herself. When she begins to exercise, the membranes tend to swell, further cutting off her air. Unless you are

**Stop and go:** This game is a training exercise in disguise. You will teach your Frenchie to sit (see page 38) and then reward her for sitting faster and faster and for staying for various lengths of time. Then you will say, *"Yippee!"* and encourage her to go wild, skittering around the house like a Frenchie possessed. Then suddenly call out *"Sit!"* Alternate sitting and running amok. How can this be training? Besides being fun, it is the best way to teach your dog to calm down quickly.

**Balloon bounce:** Take a package of balloons, blow them up, throw them up into the air, and let the fun begin! Just be sure your dog does not eat any she pops. You can also buy special dog soap bubbles that will not burn her eyes when she pops them.

## Identification

Your Frenchie should always wear a collar with identification. If you are on the road, be sure to also add a phone number where you can be reached if she should be lost out of town. Do not stop there; collars have a habit of coming off.

Your Frenchie should have a microchip, a pellet the size of a rice grain that is injected under the skin over the shoulders. Your veterinarian does this in a second. Veterinarians and shelters own scanners that read the data from the chip; that information will include contact numbers for you should your dog be found.

planning on water sports, play indoor games when the weather gets warm. Even in cool weather, bring plenty of cool water and always have a plan for getting her cooled off quickly. Don't expect her to swim, either. She will sink.

## Travel

Who could ask for a better copilot than a French Bulldog? She will never change the radio station, and she will never tease you when you get lost. She will consider the scenery around the neighborhood as enthralling as the Grand Canyon. However, you will not be so thrilled with her if she is jumping all over you, trying to make you crash just because she saw a squirrel out your side of the car. Nor will your trip be enhanced if she is drooling and puking or experiencing explosive diarrhea. The solution is simple: a travel crate!

A crate prevents her from making you get into a wreck, saves her life if you do have an accident, cuts down on carsickness, and confines diarrhea. It also lets you open your windows slightly while you are gone, although you should padlock the crate shut and lock the

car if you leave a large opening in the window. Carsickness can also be lessened by short practice trips to fun locations and by motion sickness medication. Besides water, do not forget your Frenchie's food, medication, bed, leash, collar, plastic bags, and paper towels—lots of them!

Keeping cool: If you are traveling in even moderately warm weather, bring a cooler and plenty of ice packs as well as water spray bottles. You can buy cooler crate pads filled with gel that keeps cool for hours. You should also bring a small fan that is powered through your cigarette lighter or, better, its own battery. What if your car died and you were stranded roadside without air-conditioning in the summer heat? Ice packs and battery fans could be the difference between life and death for your Frenchie.

If you are visiting friends or even staying at a motel, bring your crate inside with you. Your dog will appreciate the familiar den, and your friends will too. Do not ever leave her unattended in a strange room.

Clean up: No matter where you go, be sure to clean up after your dog. A simple poop disposal bag is a baby diaper disposal bag or a sandwich bag. Put your hand into it, pick up the poop, turn the bag inside out, and dispose.

## Destinations

Ready to get out of the house but do not know where your dog is welcome? Consider organizing a play group with your friends, neighbors, or fellow members of your training or conformation club. Find an outdoor café and do lunch together. Volunteer at a meet and greet, an event in which dogs of various breeds meet the public. Arrange a charity event, perhaps a doggy carnival or other doggy event.

Dog parks are the in thing in many cities. They can be great places for dogs to play together and run in a safely enclosed area. Remember, your Frenchie is smaller than most dogs. Do not let her run with a group of large dogs, no matter how friendly. It only takes an inadvertent bump, especially if the excitement level is already high, for several dogs to pile on a little dog. At the same time, do not let your dog be a French bully. Frenchies have a tendency to be pushy, and your dog could be scaring another dog if you let her chase and bark.

If you do travel farther afield in quest of adventure, plan ahead. Many big city hotels cater to canine clientele, and even some resort motels offer special hospitality to canine guests. You can go to a dog-friendly beach, a dude ranch, or even a dog paddling canoe adventure.

How about camp? Unlike kid's camps, you get to go too! Your Frenchie can try out all sorts of dog sports, go hiking, or just lounge around and be sociable. Some camps specialize

## Boarding

Sometimes you just cannot take her with you. If you are traveling in hot weather, taking your dog along may not just be inconvenient as you find you cannot stop to shop or see local attractions. It could be dangerous because even running into the rest stop for a minute may let her overheat in the car. So you must find a way to care for your Frenchie while you are away. Bonded pet sitters will come to your home once or twice a day to feed her and let her out. That will give your dog the security of being in her own home, but she may not get a lot of attention. A boarding kennel can be hectic. However, if she does not mind noise and other dogs, she may enjoy herself. Look for a kennel that is a member of the American Boarding Kennel Association and one that will allow you to inspect the premises and to bring her toys and bedding. Each dog should have a separate run with indoor climate-controlled living space—that means air-conditioning in even moderately warm weather. Ideally, somebody will be on the premises 24 hours a day. Some kennels even offer activities and day care.

## The Freudian Frenchie

You know how your Frenchie picks up your spirits when you are down. Have you considered sharing her antics and affection with somebody who has no access to a dog? It could be a visit to a shut-in neighbor, a nursing home resident, or a hospitalized child. You could educate schoolchildren on dog care or entertain challenged children. To become an official therapy dog, you will need to get some instruction and your dog will need to demonstrate that she is gentle, well mannered, and tolerant of what can sometimes become heavy petting. Of course, she will also need to be clean before visiting! Sharing your Frenchie is one of the most rewarding activities the two of you can pursue.

in certain skills, whereas others just specialize in fun.

**Suffering from Frenchie withdrawal?** Attend the French Bulldog Club of America National Specialty Show, where you will see hundreds of the finest and smartest Frenchies from around the country. Or go to a local Frenchie specialty show instead. Contact the club and make sure they will allow an unentered dog to attend as a spectator.

The following are some of the main points of the French Bulldog standard. Visit the French Bulldog Club of America web site for the complete standard, *www.fbdca.org*.

**General Appearance:** Compactly built, muscular dog of medium-to-small size with an alert, curious expression.

**Size:** Weight must not exceed 28 pounds (12.7 kg).

**Coat:** Short, smooth, and moderately fine. Skin is soft and loose, forming wrinkles, especially at the head and shoulders.

**Color:** All-brindle, fawn, white, brindle and white, and any color except the following: solid black, mouse, liver, black and tan, black and white, and white with black. Note: black means black without a trace of brindle.

**Gait:** Free and vigorous with reach and drive. Double tracking, meaning the legs do not converge to move along the same center line when trotting.

**Temperament:** Well behaved, adaptable, and comfortable with an affectionate nature and even disposition. Active, alert, and playful but not unduly boisterous.

- Any alteration other than removal of dewclaws.
- Weight over 28 pounds (12.7 kg).
- Ears other than bat ears.
- Nose other than black, except lighter-colored dogs may have a lighter-colored nose.
- Solid black, mouse, liver, black and tan, black and white, and white with black.

Females do not bear the characteristics of the breed to the same degree as do males. This means they are somewhat understated versions, with slighter build and a less massive head and body.

Large and square. The skull is flat between the ears, and the forehead is slightly rounded. The muzzle is broad, deep, and very short.

Well-defined, causing a hollow groove between the eyes. Heavy wrinkles form a soft fold over the muzzle.

Black. Broad nostrils with a well-defined line between them.

Thick, broad, and black, hanging over the lower jaws on the sides and covering the teeth in front.

Deep, square, broad, with an undershot bite.

Round, dark eyes of moderate size, set as far from ears as possible (wide and low in skull), and neither sunken nor bulging. Neither the haw (nictitating membrane or third eyelid) nor white of the eye should show when the dog is looking forward.

Bat ears, broad at base, elongated with a round tip. Set high on the head and facing forward. Fine, soft leather.

Thick, well-arched neck with loose skin at the throat.

Roached (arched), strong, and short; broad at shoulders and narrowing at loins.

Broad and deep.

Tucked up.

Short, hung low, thick root and fine tip, carried low at rest; may be either straight or screwed (but not in a curl).

Short, stout, straight, muscular, and set well apart. Dewclaws may be removed.

Moderate sized, with compact toes with high knuckles and short, stubby nails.

Strong and muscular, longer than forelegs so the loins are higher than the shoulders.

Well let down.

Same as front feet but slightly longer.

# Keeping Up Appearances

Your Frenchie may not need to visit the beauty parlor for the latest French cut, but he does need a little assistance in looking his best. Much of his beauty comes from inside—in this case not just his personality but his health and nutrition. What you do every day affects his health and appearance.

## COAT AND SKIN CARE

Frenchies are basically wash-and-wear dogs. They need brushing about once a week, although they will love getting it more often. You can use a soft bristle brush most times, but add a rubber shedding brush during heavy shedding. You can also hasten shedding by washing your dog in warm water and brushing him again when his coat is almost dry.

Bathing a Frenchie is easy, at least compared with other dogs. Use a dog shampoo rather than a human one because dog shampoos are formulated for the dog's skin pH of 7.5 as opposed to the human pH of 5.5. Your veterinarian carries a variety of good-quality shampoos, including some formulated for special skin conditions. For example, oatmeal-based shampoos can help soothe itchy skin, and antiseborrheic ones can decrease greasiness from seborrhea. Pick up a rinse-free shampoo for quick fixes when your dog just needs a spot bath.

For a real bath, fill a tub or sink with water the same temperature you would want to bathe in and place a nonskid mat onto the bottom. Use a spray attachment to wet the dog all over. Mix shampoo with water and massage it into the coat, making sure you do not get shampoo in his eyes. Rinse starting at the head and working down and back. You can discourage your dog from shaking water all over you by holding one of his ears. You can apply a conditioner for a softer coat. Towel dry him and take him to a warm area. He will run around in a Frenchie frenzy at first, so keep him off slippery floors. In cold weather you may want to hasten drying with a blow-dryer, but never lock your Frenchie in a cage and aim one at him. This is a recipe

for overheating, one that has cost many dogs their lives.

If you are grooming for a dog show, you can also tidy the hair inside the ears so they will look larger. You may elect to trim the vibrissae (whiskers), although many people contend that they should be left intact.

Weekly requirement: Frenchies do have one grooming need that you will need to attend to at least weekly—inspecting and cleaning their wrinkles, especially the folds on the muzzle. Skin folds can trap moisture and

bacteria and may become infected and smelly. Prevent this by cleaning the folds with an antibacterial wipe or just a paper towel dipped into warm water, and then thoroughly drying the folds. Cream Frenchies seem to need wrinkle cleaning more often. The drier you keep them throughout the week, the fewer problems you will have.

Noses: Frenchie noses often get dried and cracked. A dab of petroleum jelly or vitamin E liquid massaged on the nose once a week is usually sufficient to keep the nose soft and pliable.

Some Frenchies have weepy eyes, which will cause tear stain on the fur where they drain. Your veterinarian may be able to find a cause, such as a clogged tear duct or scratched cornea. More often, though, allergies are to blame. If you cannot get to the root

of the problem, you can combat the stains only by keeping them wiped clean and dry.

## Skin Problems

A healthy coat is more enjoyable to stroke and pet. That healthy coat depends on healthy skin. Skin allergies, parasites, and infections can make your dog uncomfortable and unhealthy.

Allergies: If your Frenchie is scratching, chewing, rubbing, and licking, he may have allergies. Frenchies seem to be somewhat susceptible to skin allergies. They can be allergic to inhaled allergens, things they come into contact with, foods, or fleas. Unlike humans, where hay fever and other inhaled allergens typically cause sneezing, in dogs they more often cause itching. Food, too, can cause allergies. Signs of allergies are typically reddened, itchy skin, particularly around the ears, eyes, feet, forelegs, armpits, and abdomen. The dog may scratch, lick, and rub his torso or rump on furniture or rugs.

### Hot Spots

A hot spot, technically known as pyrotraumatic dermatitis, is an area of skin that is irritated, perhaps by a flea bite, so that the dog scratches or chews the area. It quickly becomes enlarged, infected, and painful. Treat by clipping away the hair and cleansing the area with surgical soap. Some people find that washing with Listerine gives good results. Apply an antibiotic cream, or better, an antibiotic powder. Prevent the dog from further chewing and scratching.

Allergens can be isolated with a skin test in which small amounts of allergen extracts are injected under the skin, which is then monitored for reactions. Besides avoiding allergens, some treatments are available.

The most common inhaled allergens are dander, pollen, dust, and mold. They are often seasonal. Frenchies have a very high rate of inhalant allergies resulting in skin problems, with females particularly at risk. Signs most commonly appear between one and three years of age. Treatment includes antihistamines, glucocorticoids, and hyposensitization.

Corn products have been associated with hives in some Frenchies. The most common allergy among all dogs is flea allergy dermatitis (FAD), which is an allergic reaction to the saliva that a flea injects under the skin whenever it feeds. Not only does it cause intense itching in that area but all over the dog, especially around the rump, legs, and paws. Even a single flea bite can cause severe reactions in allergic dogs.

## External Parasites

In olden days, toy dogs were used to attract fleas from their owners. Nowadays the tables are turned, and it is your job to debug your dog.

Fleas are an age-old curse that have only recently been on the losing side. In the past, dog owners sprayed their dogs and yards with poisons until it seemed the people and dogs might die before the fleas did. It was expensive, time-consuming, and potentially dangerous. Newer products have a higher initial purchase price but are cheaper in the long run because they work and they need to be reapplied only every few months. Most of these products are available only from your veterinarian, although some discount products try to sound like they work the same.

Alternate your use of products with different ingredients to lessen the chance of flea populations becoming immune.

Ticks are harder to kill. Fipronil flea products will kill ticks but not immediately. Amitraz tick collars are also effective but not perfect. Regardless, if you are in a tick-infested area, you will need to supplement by feeling your Frenchie daily for ticks (he will like the extra petting), paying close attention around his ears, neck, and between his toes. To remove a tick, use a tissue or tweezers, and grasp the tick as close to the skin as possible. Pull slowly, trying not to lose the head or squeeze the contents back into the dog. Even if you get the head with the tick, it will often leave a bump for several days.

Ticks can transmit several diseases. A vaccination is available for Lyme disease, but it

## The Fragrant Frenchie

Clean, healthy Frenchies should have a pleasant scent. If your Frenchie stinks, there is a problem. Check his wrinkles, mouth, ears, feet, anus, and genitals for infection. Check his skin for greasiness or scaliness, which could indicate seborrhea or other skin problems. Do not just push your smelly dog off your lap; fix his problem!

There is one kind of Frenchie fragrance that may send you running for your gas mask, and that is flatulence. Not all Frenchies have a gas problem. If yours is one of the gaseous ones, try a change in diet. Dairy products, high-fiber diets, or wheat-based foods can cause gas. Sometimes fatty foods and treats will cause gas. You may have to experiment to find the right foods to keep your air supply breathable.

is not advisable for dogs that do not live in Lyme-endemic areas. Of greater concern is erhlichiosis, a potentially fatal disease that cripples the immune system and often has vague symptoms. Other tick-borne diseases include Rocky Mountain spotted fever and babesiosis. Your veterinarian can order blood tests if these conditions are suspected.

Mites can also cause problems. Sarcoptic mites cause sarcoptic mange, an intensely itchy disorder that you can catch. It is often characterized by small bumps and crusts on the ear tips, abdomen, elbows, and hocks. The condition can be treated with repeated shampoos or with an injection.

Demodex mites cause demodectic mange, a noncontagious but often difficult-to-treat condition. A couple of small patches in a puppy are commonplace and will usually go away on their own. However, many such patches or a generalized condition must be treated with repeated dips or with drug therapy. Cases involving the feet can be especially difficult to cure.

Another type of mite, the ear mite, is discussed under Ear Care.

## Ear Care

Frenchie's erect and well-ventilated ear is a paragon of canine ear health. Even so, it is not immune to ear problems. Like all dogs, a Frenchie's ear canal is made up of an initial long vertical segment with an abrupt, right angle turn before reaching the ear drum. Moisture and debris can accumulate in that hidden area and cause problems.

Cleaning: More harm is done by overzealous cleaning than by no cleaning at all. If your Frenchie has gobs of debris, though, clean his ears using an ear cleanser from your veterinarian. Go outdoors, quickly squeeze the cleaner into the ear canal, and gently massage the liquid downward and squish it around. Then stand back and let him shake his head, flinging the sludge all over the place (that is why you are outside). Do not try this if the ear is red, swollen, or painful; these call for veterinary attention.

Ear problems are often signaled by head tilt, head shaking, scratching, inflammation, discharge, debris, or even circling to one side. They could be caused by infections, allergies, seborrhea, foreign bodies, or ear mites. See your veterinarian if your Frenchie starts to display any of these signs.

Ear mites are especially common in youngsters. They are contagious, so separate a dog you suspect of having them from other pets. Signs are head shaking, head tilt, and a dark coffee-ground-like buildup in the ears. They itch like mad, so you need to get right to them. Your veterinarian can prescribe eardrops or newer drug therapies.

## Nail Care

Frenchie feet support a lot of dog. They have to be at their best to do this year after year. That means the toenails must be kept trimmed. If left untrimmed, toenails can get caught in carpet loops and pulled from the nail bed. Untrimmed nails can also impact the ground with every step, displacing the normal position of the toes and causing discomfort, splaying, and even lameness. If dewclaws, those rudimentary thumbs on the wrists, are present, they are especially prone to getting caught on things and ripped out. They can even grow in a loop and back into the leg. Cut the nails!

The only problem is that Frenchies protect their feet as though they were the feet of Olympic runners. You have to convince them from the time they are babies that this is worth the treats you will be heaping on them for every nail cut. If you do this enough and avoid cutting the quick, your Frenchie will be wishing he had more toes. Use nail clippers—the guillotine type are usually easier—and be sure they are sharp. Dull clippers crush the nail and hurt. You can also use a tiny nail grinder, but do not let the heat build up.

You can see where the quick, the sensitive and potentially bleeding part of the nail, stops in several different ways. If you look under the nail you can see where the nail begins to get hollow; anywhere it looks hollow

is quickless. In this same area, the nail will suddenly get much thinner. Again, you can safely cut the nail where it is thin. In a light-colored nail, you can see a redder area that indicates the blood supply; the sensitive quick extends slightly further down the nail than the blood supply. When in doubt, cut too little and gradually whittle your way higher. You will eventually goof and cut the quick. That calls for styptic powder (available from pet supply outlets) to quell the bleeding and lots of extra treats to assuage your guilt!

## Dental Care

Frenchies shed their baby (deciduous) teeth between four and seven months of age. Sometimes some of them, especially the canine teeth, do not fall out and the permanent teeth grow in alongside them. If the two coexist for more than a day or two, ask your veterinarian to extract the baby teeth. Otherwise, the deciduous teeth can displace the permanent teeth and affect the occlusion.

Dental care begins in puppyhood as you teach your Frenchie to enjoy getting his teeth brushed. You can use a soft bristle toothbrush and meat-flavored doggy toothpaste. Because dogs do not spit, the foaming agents in human toothpaste can make them feel sick, and the high sodium content of baking powder is unhealthy. Besides, how many people's toothpastes are meat flavored? Brush a little, and give a treat. Make it a habit to brush once a day.

Brushing a Frenchie's teeth is not as easy as brushing another breed's teeth. The teeth are hidden under those heavy hanging jowls, and they are hard to get to. If you find it impossible, the next best things are special dog foods, chews, and toys designed to inhibit tartar. Nothing, though, is as good as brushing.

Plaque and tartar spread rootward, causing irreversible periodontal disease with tissue, bone, and tooth loss. The bacteria gain an inlet to the bloodstream, where they can cause kidney and heart valve infections.

## Changing Diets

If you change from one food to another, do it gradually over several days. One of life's great mysteries is why dogs, who can seemingly scarf down garbage-can bounty without ill effects, can get upset stomachs simply by switching from one dog food to another.

Hard, crunchy foods can help, but they will not take the place of brushing. If tartar accumulates, your Frenchie may need a thorough cleaning under anesthesia. You would not think of going days, weeks, months, or even years without brushing your teeth. Why would you expect your Frenchie to?

## THE FRENCH CHEF

Every day you make a decision of momentous importance to your Frenchie's health and happiness: you choose what to put into his bowl. Years ago, that choice was simple. You just gave him what you had left over, or you fed him some dog food from the grocery store. Now you are bombarded with conflicting claims that table scraps disrupt the careful balance of commercial foods, that commercial foods are responsible for every canine ill, that you need to make your dog's food yourself, and that you cannot possibly concoct a balanced diet yourself. What is a frazzled Frenchie owner to do?

Start with the basics. Frenchies are carnivores, but they do not live by meat alone. As you know, as much as your Frenchie has a taste for meat, he will eat just about anything

in reach. His nutritional needs are best met by a diet rich in meat that also contains some vegetable matter. Meat is tastier to dogs, higher in protein, and more digestible (meaning smaller stools and fewer gas problems) than plant-based ingredients. A rule of thumb is that at least three of the first six ingredients of a dog food should be animal derived. Beyond that, you should know a little bit about nutrition.

## Nutrition

A balanced diet must have minimal amounts of protein, fat, carbohydrates, vitamins, minerals, and water.

Protein provides the building blocks for bone, muscle, coat, and antibodies. Eggs, followed by meats, have higher-quality and more digestible proteins than do plant-derived products.

Fat provides energy and aids in the transport of vitamins. Plus, it adds taste. Too little fat in the diet (less than 5 percent dry matter) results in dry coats and scaly skin. Too much fat can cause diarrhea, obesity, and a reduced appetite for more nutritious foods.

Carbohydrates abound in plant and grain ingredients. Dogs were the inventors of the low-carb diet, but people have been bulking up their dogs' food with low-cost carbohydrates for years. Dogs cannot utilize the nutrients from carbohydrates unless the carbohydrates are cooked. Even then, dogs utilize them to different degrees depending on their source. Carbohydrates from rice are best utilized, fol-

**Fiber,** such as beet pulp or rice bran, should make up a small part of the dog's diet. It is often used in weight loss diets to give the dog a full feeling, although its effectiveness is controversial. Too much fiber causes large stool volume and can impair the digestion of other nutrients.

**Water** is essential for life. It dissolves and transports other nutrients, helps regulate body temperature, and helps lubricate joints. Dehydration can cause or complicate many health problems. Keep a bowl of clean, cool water available for your Frenchie at all times.

**How much of each nutrient** should your dog get? It depends. Growing dogs need more protein, active dogs need more protein and fat, fat dogs need more protein and less fat, and sick dogs need a reduction or addition of various ingredients according to their illnesses. When comparing commercial food labels, you have to compare their dry matter. Otherwise, the higher the moisture content, the lower the nutrients' levels appear.

lowed by potato and corn, and then wheat, oat, and beans. Excessive carbohydrates in the diet can cause diarrhea, flatulence, and poor athletic performance.

**Vitamins** are essential for normal life functions. Dogs require the following vitamins in their diet: A, D, E, B1, B2, B12, niacin, pyridoxine, pantothenic acid, folic acid, and choline. Most dog foods have these vitamins added in their optimal percentages, so supplementing with vitamin tablets is rarely necessary.

**Minerals** help build tissues and organs and are part of many body fluids and enzymes. Deficiencies or excesses can cause anemia, poor growth, strange appetites, fractures, convulsions, vomiting, weakness, heart problems, and many other disorders. Again, most commercial dog foods have minerals added in their ideal percentages. Do not supplement your dog's diet with minerals, especially calcium.

## Frenchie Food Choices

Commercial dog foods should meet the Association of American Feed Control Officials' (AAFCO) guidelines for a particular age group of dogs. Almost all commercially available foods have a statement on the container certifying that the food meets AAFCO guidelines. Critics contend that these guidelines are too lenient and that many pet foods are made from substandard ingredients. Premium dog foods, available from large pet supply chains, usually use better-quality ingredients and exceed AAFCO minimums.

Commercial foods come in dry, canned, and moist varieties. Dry foods are generally the healthiest, provide needed chewing action, and are most economical, but they tend to be less appealing. Many people mix them with tastier canned foods. Canned foods are usually higher in fat and are tastier. Semimoist foods are high in sugar and, although handy for travel, lack the better attributes of the other food types. Dog treats may not always meet AAFCO requirements for a complete diet but are fine as supplements.

Home-prepared diets have become increasingly popular. Such diets have the advantage of being fresh and of using human-quality ingredients. If they are prepared according to recipes devised by certified canine nutritionists, they should have the correct proportion of nutrients. Unlike commercial dog foods, such diets are not customarily tested on generations of dogs, which makes them vulnerable to looking healthy on paper but not being properly digested or utilized by the actual dog. They can also be labor intensive, although large batches can be made and frozen.

BARF diets: Some people prefer to feed their dogs a BARF (bones and raw food) diet, with the idea that such a diet better emulates that of a wild dog. They point out that nobody ever sees wolves eating from a bag of kibble or even cooking their catch of the day. They feed raw meaty bones along with vegetables. Although dogs have better resistance to bacterial food poisoning than do humans, such diets have nonetheless occasionally been associated with food poisoning, often from salmonella, in dogs. Commercially available meats may be awash in contaminated liquids. Some sources advocate searing meat to kill surface bacteria. If you feed a raw diet, be sure you follow a recipe from a reputable source.

What about table scraps? Although too many table scraps can throw off the nutrient balance, recent research has found that dogs that eat table scraps in addition to their regular commercial diet have less incidence of gastric torsion (or "bloat"). Remember to choose your scraps carefully. Avoid hunks of fat, which can bring on pancreatitis, and avoid the following human foods that are toxic to dogs:

- Chocolate contains theobromine, a stimulant that can increase heart rate and cause seizures or even death. A lethal dose is 50 to 100 mg (.05 to .1 g) of theobromine per pound of body weight. The darker the chocolate, the more theobromine. Milk chocolate has 44 mg (0.44 g) per ounce; baker's chocolate 390 mg (.39 g).

- Xylitol, an artificial sweetener found in some gum, candy, and even toothpaste, can cause liver failure. A 25-pound (11-kg) dog that eats a gram of xylitol needs veterinary treatment.
- Onions and (to a much lesser degree) garlic destroy red blood cells, causing anemia and even death. If a dog eats more than 0.5 percent of his body weight, it can cause brownish urine, lethargy, breathlessness, diarrhea, and vomiting, even days later.
- Raisins and grapes are poisonous to some dogs. Just 0.3 ounces (8.9 ml) of grapes or 0.05 ounces (15 ml) of raisins per pound of body weight can cause kidney failure.
- Avocado can potentially cause fluid build-up in the lungs.
- Macadamia nuts can cause vomiting, weakness, fever, and muscle tremors.
- Unbaked bread dough rises inside the dog, causing bloating. The yeast in it produces alcohol, which is absorbed into the bloodstream.
- Apple seeds and stems and apricot, cherry, peach, and plum pits and stems contain cyanide, which prevents the body's cells from using oxygen. When the heart and brain are deprived of oxygen, shock and death can occur.
- Nutmeg in large amounts can cause seizures and even death.
- Coffee, especially beans or grounds, in large amounts can cause caffeine toxicity, with increased and erratic heart beats, elevated blood pressure, elevated temperature, and even seizures.
- Alcohol can make dogs drunk and even kill them.
- Spoiled or moldy food can cause food poisoning or nervous system problems. Your dog is not a trash can!

If your Frenchie eats forbidden food, make him swallow hydrogen peroxide, which should induce vomiting, and call a poison hotline or your veterinarian.

## Mealtime

One of your Frenchie's daily highlights is mealtime. Do not let him down. Make sure his meal is not only nutritious but tasty and on time. Dogs can survive on one meal a day, but your dog will be healthier if you feed him two smaller meals.

Gauge how much to feed your Frenchie by how much he eats and how much he weighs. Growing pups need a lot of food. Unless they are getting "porky," they should be allowed to eat as much as they want. If they continue eating the same amounts as they get older, they risk becoming overweight.

## Battling Bully Bulge

All dogs metabolize food at different rates, so nobody can tell you just how much to feed your dog. Your job is to monitor your dog's weight and adjust his food and exercise accordingly. You should just be able to feel (but not see) the ribs slightly when you run your hands along the rib cage. An indication of a waistline should be visible both from above and from the side—yes, even in a Frenchie.

If your Frenchie is fat, have her checked for health problems. Some disorders, such as heart disease, Cushing's disease, hypothyroidism, or the early stages of diabetes, can cause a dog to appear fat. A dog in which only the abdomen is enlarged is especially suspect and should be examined by a veterinarian. A bloated belly in a puppy may signal internal parasites.

For fat Frenchies, feed smaller portions of a lower-calorie food. Commercially available diet foods supply about 15 percent fewer calories compared with standard foods. Protein levels should remain moderate to high to avoid muscle loss when dieting. It is hard to resist those pleading eyes when your Frenchie begs for a treat, but treats add up to lots of calories during the day. If you hand over the remains of your ice cream cone, some pizza crusts, and a few pretzels that fell on the floor, that is a sizable part of a small dog's daily caloric allotment. You will need to cut down on his regular non-junk food to make up for the treats, and that is not a healthy diet. Substitute carrot sticks or rice cakes for fattening treats. Keep him away from where you prepare or eat human meals. Instead of feeding him leftovers when you are through eating, go for a walk. It will do you both good!

What about thin Frenchies? Is there such a thing? Occasionally, yes. A thin Frenchie should be checked by the veterinarian. Unexplained weight loss can be caused by heart disease, cancer, or any number of endocrine problems. If your Frenchie checks out normal, you may be able to change his diet to improve his weight. Feed more meals of a higher-calorie food. Add canned food, ground beef, or a small amount of chicken fat. Heating the food will often increase its appeal. Add a late night snack; many dogs seem to have their best appetites late at night. Beware of catering too much to your dog's whims, or you will create a finicky Frenchie!

## Special Diets

Several diseases can be helped by feeding specially formulated diets. Such diets can greatly add to a sick dog's quantity and quality of life, but often dogs grow tired of them quickly. By understanding what ingredients must be avoided in a particular illness, you may be able to include some treats in the diet as well.

**Food allergies:** Frenchies that are allergic to food ingredients are typically allergic to particular proteins. Beef and corn are common culprits. By feeding a bland diet of proteins the dog has never eaten, such as venison, duck, or rabbit, the allergic symptoms (which range from diarrhea to itchiness) should subside. If they do, ingredients are added back one by

one until an ingredient is found that triggers the response. You may have to keep your dog on a diet of novel proteins forever—at least until he develops an allergy to them and you must move to another novel protein. Some hypoallergenic diets consist not of novel proteins but of protein molecules that are too small to cause allergic reactions.

**Urinary stones:** Dogs that tend to form urinary stones may be helped by diets high in certain minerals. Such diets are also usually high-fiber diets. Because there are several types of urinary stone, your veterinarian can suggest which diet is appropriate.

**Diabetes mellitus:** Diabetic dogs need diets high in complex carbohydrates. They also need to be fed on a strict schedule.

**Liver disease:** Dogs with liver disease must eat in order to get better. However, they should avoid meat and instead get their protein from milk (unless it causes diarrhea) or soy products. They need small meals of complex carbohydrates frequently throughout the day. Vitamin A and copper levels must be kept low.

**Pancreatitis:** Pancreatitis is often precipitated by a high-fat meal, especially in older, fatter dogs. They need to be fed a low-fat diet to lessen the likelihood of recurrence.

**Congestive heart failure:** Dogs with heart failure require a low-sodium diet (bal-

anced with potassium) in order to lower their blood pressure. This will help reduce the accumulation of fluid in the lungs or abdomen.

Kidney disease: Diets for kidney disease should have moderate quantities of high-quality protein. Proteins produce toxic wastes that impaired kidneys cannot clear, causing the dog to feel ill. By feeding higher-quality protein, such as eggs (especially egg whites), beef, or chicken, the fewest toxic by-products are produced in comparison with protein used.

Lower levels of high-quality protein will make the dog feel better in advanced kidney failure. Controlling phosphorus, common in meats and cheeses, is an essential part of diet management. Sodium must also be kept low. Feeding a high-fat diet will add essential calories.

Prescription diets are available through your veterinarian for all these conditions. In addition, your veterinarian can give you recipes for home-prepared diets that meet these requirements.

# French Bulldog Health

Frenchies are like humans, so even they get sick once in a while. By knowing the signs of illness, when to call the veterinarian, and how to be a doggy nurse, you can help your Frenchie stay healthy.

# A CLEAN BULL OF HEALTH

Do not wait until your dog is sick to choose a veterinarian. Consider availability, emergency arrangements, facilities, costs, ability to communicate, and experience with Frenchies, Bulldogs, or other brachycephalic breeds. Most general veterinarians can provide a wide range of services. However, if your dog has a problem that eludes diagnosis or requires specialized treatment, let your veterinarian know if you are willing to be referred to a specialist in that field.

Being the link between your dog and her doctor is not an easy job. Since your dog cannot talk, you have to interpret her behavioral and physical signs.

## Behavior Changes

Sick dogs often lie quietly in a curled position. Irritability, restlessness, hiding, clawing, panting, and trembling may indicate pain. Dogs with abdominal pain often stretch and bow. A dog with breathing difficulties will often refuse to lie down or if she does, will keep her head raised. Confusion, head pressing, or seizures may indicate neurological problems.

Lethargy is the most common sign of illness. Possible causes include:

- Infection (check for fever)
- Anemia (check gum color)
- Circulatory problem (check pulse and gum color)
- Pain (check limbs, neck, back, mouth, eyes, ears, and abdomen for signs)
- Nausea
- Poisoning (check gum color and pupil reaction; look for vomiting or abdominal pain)
- Sudden vision loss
- Cancer
- Metabolic diseases

## Intake and Output Changes

Changes in eating, drinking, or elimination patterns often indicate illness. Loss of appetite is most often associated with illness, although increased appetite may accompany some endocrine disorders. Increased thirst, usually with increased urination, may indicate kidney disease or diabetes.

The sudden and frequent urge to urinate, usually in small amounts and often accompanied by signs of pain, may indicate a urinary tract infection. Painful urination, straining to urinate, or blood in the urine may indicate urinary stones. Inability to urinate is a life-threatening emergency.

Regurgitating food right after eating can indicate an esophageal problem (see page 85).

## Frenchies and Anesthesia

Anesthesia is never taken lightly in any breed, but it is even more of a concern in Frenchies. Many procedures that would require anesthesia in more excitable or wimpy breeds can be done in wide-awake Frenchies. Your veterinarian should be aware of the following anesthesia advice. Frenchies are hard to intubate, and they require a shorter endotracheal tube than might be guessed from their size. They appear to require less anesthesia than other dogs of comparable size. A Frenchie should remain intubated until she is awake and should spend her recovery on her stomach to lessen the chance her soft palate or large tongue will block the airway. Swelling in the pharynx or larynx, which can occur with intubation, can be very serious. If your veterinarian is not experienced anesthetizing Frenchies or other brachycephalic breeds, ask for a referral to one who is.

Vomiting food after it has been in the stomach can indicate poisoning, blockage, or a host of problems. Consult your veterinarian immediately if your dog vomits feces-like matter (which could indicate an intestinal blockage) or blood (which may resemble coffee grounds), has accompanying fever or pain, or if the vomiting lasts more than a few hours.

Diarrhea can result from nervousness, a change in diet or water, food sensitivities, intestinal parasites, infections, poisoning, or many illnesses. It is not uncommon for dogs to have blood in their diarrhea. However, diarrhea with lots of blood or accompanied by vomiting, fever, or other symptoms of illness warrants a call to the veterinarian. Bright-red blood indicates a source lower in the digestive tract, while dark-black, tarry stools indicate a source higher in the digestive tract.

## Coughing

Coughing can be caused by foreign bodies, tracheal collapse, tumors, kennel cough, and heart disease, among others. Congestive heart failure causes coughing and breathing difficulties mainly after exercise, at night, and in early morning. Kennel cough is a communicable airborne disease caused by several infectious agents. It is characterized by a gagging or honking cough, often a week after being around infected dogs. Gagging, snorting, coughing up froth, or pawing at the throat may be signs of brachycephalic syndrome (see page 83). Any cough lasting longer than a few days or accompanied by weakness or difficulty breathing warrants a veterinary exam.

## Physical Changes

Sometimes you need to check over your dog piece by piece.

Mouth: If you think your Frenchie is sick, one of the first things to check is her gum color. Gums should be a deep pink. If you press with your thumb, they should return to pink within two seconds after lifting your thumb (a longer time suggests a circulatory problem). Very pale gums may indicate anemia, shock, or poor circulation. Bluish gums or tongue can mean a life-threatening lack of oxygen. Bright-red gums may indicate overheating or carbon monoxide poisoning, and yellow gums may mean jaundice. Tiny red splotches may indicate a blood-clotting problem. Tooth and gum problems will often cause bad breath and pain.

**Nose:** A nasal discharge may indicate a respiratory illness or other disease, or a foreign body or infection of the nose. A cracked nose pad may just be an overly dry nose that needs to be moisturized, or it could be caused by a disease. Pinched nostrils can cause breathing difficulties (see page 83).

**Eyes:** Squinting or pawing at the eye can arise from pain. Swelling and redness may indicate glaucoma, a scratched cornea, or several other problems. Profuse tear discharge may be caused by a foreign body, scratched cornea, or blocked tear drainage duct. Thick mucus and a dull-appearing surface may indicate dry eye (keratoconjunctivitis sicca, or KCS).

Hereditary juvenile cataracts, while not common, can occur in the breed. A DNA test for the condition is available through *www.vetgen.com.*

**Ears:** Inflamed or painful ears can result from infection or parasites. See pages 66–67 for more about ears.

**Feet:** Foot problems can account for limping. Cut long or split nails short (see page 67), and protect cut pads. Swollen toes could be from an infection or an orthopedic problem.

**Skin:** Parasites, allergies, and infections can cause many skin problems (see pages 64–65). Lumps in the skin may or may not be serious but do warrant a veterinary examination. Frenchies with lighter coat colors seem to be more susceptible to certain skin infections.

**Anus:** Repeated diarrhea can cause an irritated anal area. Repeated scooting or licking can be from diarrhea, parasites, or especially, impacted anal sacs. Many Frenchies cannot reach their anal area to lick, but they may

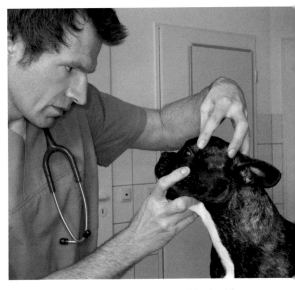

still try. The anal sacs are two sacs filled with smelly brown liquid that is normally excreted with the feces or in times of fright. In some cases, the material cannot get out. This is especially true if the tail twists sharply to one side, which can compress one duct. The sac becomes uncomfortably distended, sometimes becoming infected. It may swell outward, even appearing to be a tumor, and often finally bursting. Your veterinarian can manually express the contents.

## Temperature

To take your dog's temperature, lubricate a rectal thermometer and insert it about 2 inches (5 cm) into the dog's anus, leaving it there for about a minute. Normal is from 101°F to 102°F (38.3°C to 38.8°C). If the temperature is

- 103°F (39.4°C) or above, call your veterinarian for advice. This is not usually an emergency.
- 105°F (40.6°C) or above, go to your veterinarian. This is probably an emergency;

# The Five-Minute Checkup

Make several copies of this checklist, and keep a record of your dog's home exams.

Date: _____

Weight: _____

Temperature: _____

Pulse: _____

Behavior

Is your dog
- ☐ Restless?
- ☐ Lethargic?
- ☐ Weak?
- ☐ Dizzy?
- ☐ Irritable?
- ☐ Confused?
- ☐ Bumping into things?
- ☐ Trembling?
- ☐ Pacing?
- ☐ Hiding?
- ☐ Eating more or less than usual?
- ☐ Drinking more than usual?
- ☐ Urinating more or less than usual or with straining?
- ☐ Having diarrhea?
- ☐ Straining to defecate?
- ☐ Standing on the front legs with rear legs elevated?
- ☐ Vomiting or trying to vomit?
- ☐ Regurgitating undigested food?
- ☐ Gagging?
- ☐ Coughing?
- ☐ Breathing rapidly at rest?
- ☐ Spitting up froth?
- ☐ Pawing at throat?
- ☐ Snorting?
- ☐ Limping?

Physical Exam

Hydration: ☐ Dry, sticky gums? ☐ Skin that does not pop back when stretched?

Gum color: ☐ Pink (good) ☐ Bright red ☐ Bluish ☐ Whitish ☐ Red spots

Gums: ☐ Swellings? ☐ Bleeding? ☐ Sores? ☐ Growths?

Teeth: ☐ Loose? ☐ Painful? ☐ Dirty? ☐ Bad breath?

Nose: ☐ Thick or colored discharge? ☐ Cracking? ☐ Pinched? ☐ Sores?

Eyes: ☐ Tearing? ☐ Mucous discharge? ☐ Dull surface? ☐ Squinting? ☐ Swelling? ☐ Redness? ☐ Unequal pupils? ☐ Pawing at eyes?

Ears: ☐ Bad smell? ☐ Redness? ☐ Abundant debris? ☐ Scabby ear tips? ☐ Head shaking? ☐ Head tilt? ☐ Ear scratching? ☐ Painfulness?

Feet: ☐ Long or split nails? ☐ Cut pads? ☐ Swollen or misaligned toes?

Skin: ☐ Parasites? ☐ Black grains (flea dirt)? ☐ Hair loss? ☐ Scabs? ☐ Greasy patches? ☐ Bad odor? ☐ Lumps?

Anal and genital regions: ☐ Swelling? ☐ Discharge? ☐ Redness? ☐ Bloody urine? ☐ Bloody or blackened diarrhea? ☐ Worms in stool or around anus? ☐ Scooting rear? ☐ Licking rear?

Abdomen: ☐ Bloating?

Body: ☐ Asymmetrical bones or muscles? ☐ Lumps? ☐ Weight change?

If you answered "yes" to anything abnormal in the checklist, call your veterinarian. Refer to the text for more information.

106°F (41.1°C) or above is dangerous. Try to cool your dog.

- 98°F (36.7°C) or below, called your veterinarian for advice. Try to warm your dog.
- 96°F (35.6°C) or below, go to your veterinarian. Treat for hypothermia on the way by warming your dog.

## Pulse

To check the pulse, cup your hand around the top of your dog's rear leg so your fingers are near the top almost where the leg joins the body. Feel for the pulse in the femoral artery. Normal adult Frenchie pulse rate is 70 to 120 beats per minute.

## Hydration

Check hydration by touching the gums, which should be slick, not sticky, or by lifting the skin on the back and letting it go. It should snap back into place quickly, not remain tented. Sticky gums and tented skin indicate dehydration. If your dog has been vomiting or has diarrhea, she may instantly lose any water you give her, in which case your veterinarian may need to give your dog fluids under the skin, or better, in a vein.

## FRENCH BULLDOG HEALTH CONCERNS

Like all breeds, Frenchies are prone to certain health conditions. A survey conducted by the FBDCA Health and Genetics Committee in 2000 found the most reported specific problems were hemivertebrae (12 percent), elongated soft palate (8 percent), stenotic nares (6 percent), atopic dermatis (6 percent), retinal dysplasia (5 percent), hip dysplasia (4 percent), and disk

degeneration (4 percent). These percentages should not be taken to represent actual prevalence within the breed since they came from a small and possibly biased sample. However, the survey does give an idea of what owners consider important. Foremost among general problems perceived by owners were spinal conditions and brachycephalic syndrome.

## Spinal Conditions

The French Bulldog's conformation contributes to its susceptibility to hemivertebrae and disk degeneration. Hemivertebrae occurs most

often in dogs with screw tails, a trait that is actually a form of hemivertebrae. In hemivertebrae, the right and left halves of a vertebra do not fuse as they should, and the two halves grow unequally. This happens most often in the thoracic (T9–T11) vertebrae, where it can cause

## No Human Medicine!

Dogs and humans metabolize drugs differently. While some drugs are safe for both, others are not. Most common culprits are NSAIDs, such as ibuprofen or naproxen, which can cause stomach ulcers and kidney failure in dogs; over the counter cold medicines containing acetaminophen and cough suppressants and prescription ADD/ADHD medications can cause tremors, seizures, and cardiac problems in dogs. Always check with your veterinarian before giving human medication to your dog!

a curvature of the spine either side to side or up and down. In some cases, this causes a kink in the spine, compressing the spinal cord. In these cases, surgery may be needed to prevent partial paralysis. Screening radiographs can be done even in puppies.

**Intervertebral disk degeneration** is similar to the well-known problem in Dachshunds and some other chondrodysplastic dwarf breeds. A chondrodsyplastic breed is one, like the French Bulldog, in which the long bones of the legs fail to develop while the torso develops normally. Chondrodysplastic dwarfs are more susceptible to intervertebral disk degeneration. The intervertebral disks are the cushions between the disks. The gelatinous substance in them is abnormally fibrous in chondrodysplastic dwarf breeds. It tends to become calcified and lose its elasticity. If too much force, especially twisting force, is applied to part of a disk, it can rupture and squeeze into the area surrounding the spinal cord, compressing the cord. Prevention entails avoiding undue stress on the disks by avoiding obesity and avoiding jumping and twisting. When problems occur in fairly young Frenchies (3 to 5 year olds) they usually affect the disks of the neck (C2–C4) or thoracic-lumbar regions (T11–L2).

Signs of disk herniation depend on the location and severity. They may range from a stiff, painful neck, to an arched back and stiff gait, to crying when lifted, a wobbly gait, toe dragging, and even rear end paralysis. Quick treatment with drugs to reduce swelling and strict, prolonged cage rest is essential. Surgery may be necessary to prevent irreversible spinal cord damage. A dog with a paralyzed rear may need to use a mobility cart to support her hindquarters.

## Brachycephalic Syndrome

Dogs with flat faces tend to have compacted respiratory systems, which lead to a condition called brachycephalic syndrome. It consists of a group of anatomical abnormalities, including elongated soft palate, stenotic nares, and sometimes other abnormalities that cause breathing problems.

The soft palate is the mobile flap that extends from the rear of the roof of the mouth. Its purpose is to prevent food and water from going into the nasal passages when swallowing. When elongated, it hangs in the airway or larynx during inhalation, obstructing the airway. An affected dog may have to breathe through her mouth and may snore, snort, and gag, especially when the dog is hot or excited. The harder the dog breathes, the more the soft palate swells and the greater the obstruction. A

### Signs of Brachycephalic Syndrome

✔ Can you see or hear your dog's nostrils interfere with air intake?
✔ Does her breathing become labored in warm weather or with mild exercise?
✔ Does she gag up froth?
✔ Does she snore, snort, gag, or gurgle frequently?
✔ Does she overheat easily?

Consider having your veterinarian check your dog's palate and larynx, especially when your dog requires anesthesia for a procedure.

## Medications

✔ To give a pill, open your dog's mouth and place the pill well into the rear of her mouth. Close her mouth and gently stroke the throat until she swallows. You can also hide the pill in some cream cheese or other soft treat and watch to make sure she eats it.

✔ To give liquid medication, place the liquid into the side of her mouth and let the dog lap it down. Do not squirt it in so that the dog inhales it.

✔ Always give the full course of medications prescribed by your veterinarian.

✔ Never give human medications unless your veterinarian tells you to. Some human medications work on dogs but must be used at different strengths, and some have no effect or bad effects on dogs.

definite diagnosis may need to be made under anesthesia, at which time surgical correction is advised.

Stenotic nares, or constricted nostrils, are the result of overly soft cartilage that forms the nostrils. When the dog inhales, the nostrils collapse on themselves, shutting off the air flow. The dog may have labored breathing, mouth breathing, snorting, and a watery or foamy nasal discharge. The dog may develop a flattened chest and be in generally poor condition. Surgical treatment in which the nostrils are enlarged should be performed as soon as possible in such dogs.

Other components of brachycephalic syndrome may include tortuous turbinates, in which the pathways of the nasal airways are abnormally twisted, and a hypoplastic trachea, in which the trachea is abnormally narrow. Whether together or separately, these traits cause breathing difficulties. In turn, the increased suction required to pull air through the obstructed airway sucks the laryngeal walls and saccules (small sacs lining the larynx) into the glottis, and the increased turbulence causes the laryngeal membranes to swell. These cause further airway obstruction.

Tracheal collapse: Adding to the problem, some Frenchies have underdeveloped tracheal cartilage. Increased sucking forces can contribute to the collapse of the cartilage rings that form the trachea, flattening the trachea and dangerously obstructing air flow. This causes a goose honk kind of cough, especially when excited. In severe cases, the dog shows signs of lacking oxygen.

Airway obstruction creates a vicious cycle in which obstruction causes changes that cause even greater obstruction. Sometimes the condition gets gradually worse without the owner's notice until something—exercise, hot weather, respiratory infection—causes just enough additional swelling that the trachea totally collapses or the laryngeal saccules or soft palate totally plug the airway. The dog then asphyxiates and dies. If you suspect your Frenchie has any component of brachycephalic syndrome, do not let it go unchecked until it has spiraled out of control. If possible, have your dog evaluated and treated by a veterinarian experienced with surgical correction of these problems.

## Other Health Concerns

Breathing difficulties, overheating, and spinal problems are the Frenchie's biggest breed-associated health concerns. However, the following conditions, most of which are hereditary, are also seen at a slightly higher-than-average rate in the breed compared with most other breeds.

Patellar luxation occurs when the patella, or kneecap, slips out of place. In mild cases, the major symptom is occasionally hopping with one rear leg held forward for a few steps. In more severe cases, the dog never puts her weight on the leg. Some cases require surgical correction.

Hip dysplasia, in which the head of the femur (thigh bone) does not fit properly in the hip socket, causes the joint to be unstable, in turn leading to arthritis and pain. Although hip dysplasia occurs in Frenchies, it seldom seems to cause problems, possibly because the breed's heavy thigh muscles keep everything tight. The Orthopedic Foundation for Animals evaluates hip radiographs and maintains a registry of evaluated dogs.

Histiocytic ulcerative colitis, which is a type of inflammation of the large intestine, is seen in some families of French Bulldogs. Affected dogs have chronic diarrhea and may need long-term drug therapy.

Cleft palate: Brachycephalic dogs are more likely to be born with cleft palates, in which an opening persists between the mouth and nose. This causes difficulty nursing or eating, increased nasal infections, and general poor health. Surgery is the only treatment and is usually attempted for only relatively small clefts.

von Willebrand's disease: Many breeds of dogs, including Frenchies, may have a hereditary blood-clotting disorder called von

Willebrand's disease. It varies in its severity but can cause spontaneous or excessive bleeding.

Megaesophagus is a condition in which the esophagus is enlarged so that normal swallowing is difficult. Food is often regurgitated. Keeping food down can become so difficult that the dog becomes generally unthrifty or acquires aspiration pneumonia. Affected dogs do better if fed from a raised surface so gravity will help swallowing.

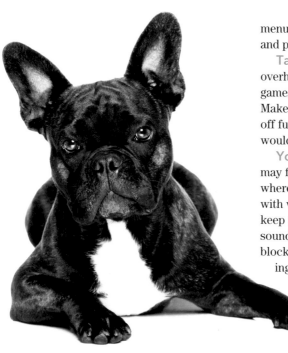

Eye and lid problems: Eye-related problems, such as juvenile cataracts (premature opacification of the lens), entropion (the eyelid turning inward), and distichiasis (abnormally placed eyelashes that rub on the eye) are sometimes reported in Frenchies.

## THE GOLDEN YEARS

Old age is the reward of good genes, good care, and good luck. French Bulldogs have an average life span of nine to eleven years, with many living into their teens. Older Frenchies still need lots of mental and physical stimulation but maybe not at the level they did as youngsters. Riding in the car, assisting with the laundry, running laps in the house, planning the menu, and daring that squirrel to come down and play can fill an older Frenchie's day.

Take extra precautions against stress, overheating, chilling, and injuries. Plan indoor games that are not too physically demanding. Make ramps so your dog can easily get on and off furniture (yes, the same furniture you swore would be off limits 10 years ago).

Your Frenchie's vision and hearing may fade, so be sure she cannot wander off where she cannot see or hear you. Frenchies with vision loss can cope well as long as you keep them in familiar surroundings, place sound or scent beacons at key locations, and block off pools and steps. Frenchies with hearing loss can learn to respond to hand signals, vibrating collars, and flashing lights using the same training techniques you used to teach voice commands.

Cognitive dysfunction: Many older dogs suffer from cognitive dysfunction, in which they appear confused, depressed, or disoriented. Challenging their minds with games or new tricks every day can help stave it off. Your veterinarian can also prescribe drug therapy that may give good results.

Excessive weight places an added burden on the heart, back, and joints, but keeping an older Frenchie svelte can be a challenge. Most healthy older Frenchies do not need a special diet, but they should receive high-quality protein. Moistening dry food or adding canned food can help dogs with dental problems enjoy their meals.

Dental problems: Now is the time to address any dental problems. Bad breath, lip licking, reluctance to chew, or swelling around the mouth can all signal periodontal disease. A thorough tooth cleaning and perhaps drug therapy is needed.

Do not ignore strong body odors, which can signal periodontal disease, impacted anal sacs, seborrhea, or ear infections. Regular brushing can help soothe dry, itchy skin by stimulating oil production. The nails tend to get especially long in older dogs, so you will need to cut them more often.

Other health issues: A senior Frenchie should have a checkup twice a year. That is not excessive when you consider the rate at which they are aging. Tests can detect early stages of treatable diseases.

Arthritis slows many older dogs. Keeping weight down, providing a warm, soft bed, attending to injuries, and maintaining a program of low-impact exercise can help mild cases. Drugs and supplements can also help. Polysulfated glycosaminoglycan increases the compressive resilience of cartilage. Glucosamine stimulates collagen synthesis and may help rejuvenate cartilage; and chondroitin sulfate helps shield cartilage from destructive enzymes. Anti-inflammatory drugs may help alleviate some pain but must be used with veterinary supervision.

Older dogs may have less efficient immune systems, making it more important to shield them from infectious diseases or stress. However, if your Frenchie stays home all the time, she may not need to be vaccinated as often as when she was younger. This is an area of controversy that you should discuss with your veterinarian.

Dogs suffer from many of the same diseases of old age that humans do. Cancer accounts for almost half the deaths of dogs over the age of 10 years. Its signs include weight or appetite loss, collapse, swellings, lameness, difficulty swallowing, or lethargy, among others. Heart disease, often signaled by weakness, coughing, or fluid accumulation in the tissues of the limbs or belly, is also a major problem of older dogs. Kidney disease, signaled by increased thirst and urination, is yet another major problem. Cushing's syndrome (hyperadrenocorticism) is also seen more often in older dogs. Its signs include increased hunger, thirst, and urination as well as hair loss, muscle atrophy, and a potbelly. Your veterinarian can diagnose and treat most of these problems.

First aid does not take the place of veterinary attention. In every case below, first call the veterinarian, and then apply first aid as you are transporting the dog. Move the dog as little as possible, but get her in a safe place. Be ready to treat for shock.

## Shock

Signs of shock are weakness, collapse, pale gums, unresponsiveness, and faint pulse. Since it may occur in almost any case of trauma, it is usually best to treat the dog as though she were in shock. Keep her warm and quiet, and keep her head low compared with her heart (unless she has a head wound).

## Heat Stroke

Early signs of heat stroke include rapid loud breathing, abundant thick saliva, bright-red mucous membranes, and high rectal temperature. Later signs include unsteadiness, diarrhea, and coma.

Wet the dog down and place her in front of a fan. If this is not possible, immerse her in cold water. Do not plunge her into ice water, because that constricts the peripheral blood vessels so much that they cannot cool the blood as well. Offer water to drink.

You must lower your dog's body temperature quickly, but do not let the temperature go below 100°F (37.8°C). Stop cooling when the rectal temperature reaches 103°F (39.4°C) because it will continue to fall.

Even when the temperature is back to normal, your Frenchie is still in danger and still needs veterinary attention. Your dog will take several days to recover, during which she should not exert herself.

## Bleeding

To control bleeding, cover the wound with a clean dressing and apply pressure. Apply more dressing over any blood-soaked ones until the bleeding stops. Elevating the wound site and applying a cold pack to the wound area will also slow bleeding. If the wound is on the front leg, apply pressure to the inside of the front leg just above the elbow. If it is on the rear leg, apply pressure inside the thigh where the femoral artery crosses the thighbone.

## Stings

Insect stings can sometimes cause allergic reactions. Swelling around the nose and throat can block the airways. Other possible reactions include restlessness, vomiting, diarrhea, seizures, and collapse. At the slightest hint of a reaction, give an allergy pill (ask your veterinarian for the best type to keep in your first aid kit and how much to give).

A dog having a seizure may drool, stiffen, yelp, or twitch uncontrollably. Wrap the dog in a blanket, and keep her away from stairs and other dogs. Never put your hands or anything into a convulsing dog's mouth. Make note of everything you can remember about the seizure, which may help determine the cause.

Signs of poisoning vary according to the type of poison but often include vomiting, depression, and convulsions. When in doubt, call your veterinarian or an animal poison control hotline. If the poison was ingested in the past two hours and if it is not an acid, alkali, petroleum product, solvent, or tranquilizer, you may be advised to induce vomiting by giving hydrogen peroxide or dry mustard mixed 1:1 with water. Ipecac syrup is not recommended for this purpose in dogs. In other cases, you may be advised to dilute the poison by giving milk or vegetable oil. Activated charcoal can absorb many toxins. Poisons act in different ways, so you need to have the label of any suspected poisons available.

Ethylene-glycol-based antifreeze is a dog killer. Even tiny amounts cause irreversible kidney damage, and the prognosis is poor once symptoms appear. Get emergency help if you suspect your dog drank antifreeze.

Rodent poisons are either warfarin based, which cause uncontrolled internal bleeding, or cholecalciferol based, which cause kidney failure.

Bird and squirrel poisons are usually strychnine based, which cause neurological malfunction.

Insect poisons, weed killers, and wood preservatives may be arsenic based, which cause kidney failure.

Flea, tick, and internal parasite poisons may contain organophosphates, which can cause neurological symptoms.

Iron-based rose fertilizers can cause kidney and liver failure.

## The First Aid Kit

✔ Emergency veterinary phone number
✔ First aid instructions
✔ Rectal thermometer
✔ Scissors
✔ Sterile gauze dressings
✔ Self-adhesive bandage
✔ Antiseptic skin ointment
✔ Instant cold compress
✔ Antidiarrheal medication
✔ Allergy medication
✔ Ophthalmic ointment
✔ Penlight
✔ Hydrogen peroxide
✔ Activated charcoal
✔ Tongue depressor
✔ Soap

Information

## Organizations

French Bulldog Club of America
*www.fbdca.org*

French Bulldog Club of America Charitable
Fund
*www.fbdca/cf*

Canine Health Foundation
*www.akcchf.org*

Orthopedic Foundation for Animals
*www.offa.org*

Therapy Dogs International
*www.tdi-dog.org*

## Local French Bulldog Clubs

French Bulldog Club of Arizona
*www.frenchbulldogclubofarizona.com/index.
html*

French Bulldog Club of Dallas/Ft. Worth
*www.frenchbulldogclubdfw.com*

French Bulldog Club of Puget Sound
*www.thefrenchbulldogclubofpugetsound.org*

French Bulldog Fanciers of Mid-Florida
*www.frenchbulldogfanciersofmidfl.com*

French Bulldog Fanciers of Southern
California
*www.frenchiesfirst.com*

Great Lakes French Bulldog Club
*www.glfbc.webs.com*

Heart of Texas French Bulldog Club
*www.hotfrenchbulldogs.com*

Heartland French Bulldog Club
*www.heartlandfrenchbulldogclub.org*

Mason Dixon French Bulldog Club
*www.facebook.com/pages/Mason-Dixon-
French-Bulldog-Club*

Northern California French Bulldog Club
*www.ncfbc.com*

Pacific NW French Bulldog Club
*www.pnwfbc.org*

French Bulldog Fanciers of Southern California
*www.frenchiesfirst.com*

## Breeder Listings

AKC Breeder Classified
*www.akc.org/classified*

French Bulldog Club of America Breeder Listing
Service
*www.frenchbulldogclub.org/about-frenchies/
breeder-listing*

## Rescue

French Bulldog Rescue on Facebook
*www.facebook.com/FrenchBulldogRescue*

French Bulldog Village
*www.frenchbulldogvillage.net*

## Periodicals

Frenchies Online
*www.FrenchiesOnline.com*

*The French Bullytin*
*www.frenchbullytin.com*

Just Frenchies
*www.JustFrenchies.com*

## Books

Alford, Arlie, Jane Flowers, Michael Rosser, and Ann Winsor. *Celebrating Frenchies.* ArDesign, Mendota, MN, 2004.

Coile, D. Caroline. *Beyond Fetch: Fun, Interactive Activities for You and Your Dog.* Wiley, New York, NY, 2003.

Coile, D. Caroline. *Show Me! A Dog Showing Primer.* Barron's Educational Series, Inc., Hauppauge, NY, 1997.

Eltinge, Steve. *The French Bulldog.* MIP Publishing, Santa Barbara, CA, 1988.

Grebe, Janice. *Healthy Frenchies: An Owner's Manual.* ArDesign, Mendota, MN, 1998.

Grebe, Janice and Stephen Eltinge. *Flat Face Encyclopedia—Bulldogs and French Bulldogs: A To Z.* ArDesign, Mendota, MN, 1997.

Lee, Muriel. *The French Bulldog.* Kennel Club Books, Freehold, NJ, 2007.

Visit *www.frenchbullytin.com/Publications. html* for more books.

## Videos

AKC Breed Standard Video
*www.akc.org/store/*

## Web Pages

French Bulldog Kingdom
*www.frenchbulldog.com/*

French Bulldog Z
*www.frenchbulldogz.net*

Infodog Dog Show Site
*www.infodog.com*

## Important Note

This pet owner's manual tells the reader how to buy or adopt, and care for, a French Bulldog. The author and publisher consider it important to point out that the advice given in the book is meant primarily for normally developed dogs of excellent physical health and sound temperament.

Anyone who acquires a fully-grown dog should be aware that the animal has already formed its basic impressions of human beings. The new owner should watch the animal carefully, including its behavior toward humans, and, whenever possible, should meet the previous owner.

Caution is further advised in the association of children with dogs, in meeting with other dogs, and in exercising the dog without a leash.

Even well-behaved and carefully supervised dogs sometimes do damage to someone else's property or cause accidents. It is therefore in the owner's interest to be adequately insured against such eventualities, and we strongly urge all dog owners to purchase a liability policy that covers their dog.

# Index

## About the Author

Caroline Coile is an award-winning author who has written numerous articles about dogs for both scientific and lay publications. Her writing credits also include many well-respected books on the various aspects of dogs and dog sports. She holds a Ph.D. in neuroscience and behavior with special interests in canine sensory systems, genetics, and behavior. An active dog fancier since 1963, her own dogs have been nationally ranked in conformation, obedience, and performance activities.

## Cover Photos

Shutterstock: front cover: AnetaPics: top right; Eric Isselee: main; VKarlov: middle right; WilleeCole Photography: bottom right; back cover: Eric Isselee; inside front and back covers: Patryk Kosmider

## Photo Credits

123rf: arnoaltix: page 38
Daniel Johnson: page 45 (top)
Dreamstime: Daniela Jakob: page 53
fotolia: biglama: page 77; Christoph Hähnel: pages 79, 81; drubig-photo: page 29; Ingus Evertovskis: page 58; littleevilyorky: page 83; Natane: page 57 (bottom); Patryk Kosmider: pages 44, 54; WilleeCole Photography: page 47
iStock: Den Guy: page 67; druvo: pages 22, 24; JMichl: page 63
Patty Sosa: page 60
Shutterstock: AnetaPics: pages 41, 48, 50, 57 (top); Tatiana Katsai: pages 27, 49; Rita Kochmarjova: pages 2, 4, 13, 16, 20, 36, 75, 85; Dora Zett: pages 3, 31, 71, 72; Dragon Images: page 59; Eric Isselee: pages 5, 19, 28, 42, 45 (bottom), 51, 70, 82, 87; Dorte Vilsgaard: page 10; Grisha Bruev: page 9; Jagodka: pages 11, 34, 40, 68, 91; Javier Brosch: page 86; JLSnader: page 33; Liliya Kulianionak: pages 15, 21, 93; Kachalkina Veronika: page 88; Kitch Bain: page 74; Kwiatek7: pages 56, 62, 90, 92; Matteo Dini: page 35; Michal Nowosielski: page 39; Patryk Kosmider: page 73; pixbull: page 23; Robert Neumann: page 69; Robynrg: page 37; Tatiana katsai: page 6; Thaworn Kimtong: page 18; Tomasz Guzowski: page 12; tsik: pages 46, 65; WilleeCole Photography: pages 30, 32, 43, 64, 76

## Acknowledgments

The author is indebted to Kathy Waller and Luis Sosa for their valuable contributions to the text. Special thanks to Seymour Weiss for his editorial and canine expertise.

*All inquiries should be addressed to:*
Barron's Educational Series, Inc.
250 Wireless Boulevard
Hauppauge, NY 11788
**www.barronseduc.com**

ISBN: 978-1-4380-0486-0

Library of Congress Control Number: 2014946545

Printed in China
9 8 7 6 5 4 3 2 1